A CLEVELAND

RECIPES FROM THE JUNIOR LEAGUE OF CLEVELAND, INC.

PUBLISHED BY

THE JUNIOR LEAGUE OF CLEVELAND, INC.
CLEVELAND, OHIO

PHOTOGRAPHY

JOHN GODT, MG STUDIOS, INC.

DESIGN

KAREN DONOVAN GODT, MG STUDIOS, INC.

League House

A Cleveland Collection is a culmination of the many talents and endless hours given by the volunteers of The Junior League of Cleveland, Inc. The main ingredient of this book is "dedication"... dedication to an organization and a city in which we believe.

The purpose of this book is to showcase the City of Cleveland and to raise funds for the projects supported by The Junior League of Cleveland, Inc. We are a community of diverse cultures and living styles. When blended, we are the flavor of Cleveland.

Enjoying food is a tradition we all share in celebrating life. Preparing food can be a necessity, recreation or an art.

We hope this book enhances your appetite, your cooking adventures and your appreciation of Cleveland, Ohio.

TABLE of CONTENTS

The Junior League of Cleveland, Inc. is an organization of women committed to promoting voluntarism and to improving the community through the effective action and leadership of trained volunteers. Its purpose is exclusively educational and charitable.

The Junior League of Cleveland, Inc. reaches out to women of all races, religions, and national origins who demonstrate an interest in and a commitment to voluntarism.

The proceeds realized from the sale of **A CLEVELAND COLLECTION** will be returned to the community through projects supported by The Junior League of Cleveland, Inc.

WINE INFORMATION
PAT O'BRIEN
PAT O'BRIEN'S FINE WINES
PEPPER PIKE, OHIO

NUTRITIONAL ANALYSIS
THE CLEVELAND CLINIC FOUNDATION
CLEVELAND, OHIO

RECIPE EDITOR
MARGARET ANN GIBSON

PRINTER
EMERSON PRESS
CLEVELAND, OHIO

Additional copies of
A CLEVELAND COLLECTION may be obtained by writing:

A Cleveland Collection
The Junior League of Cleveland, Inc.
10819 Magnolia Drive
Cleveland, Ohio 44106
(216) 231-1019

Please enclose your return address with a check payable to
A CLEVELAND COLLECTION - JLC in the amount of $24.95 per book plus
$5 for postage and handling. Ohio residents sales tax, $1.75 each.

The Junior League of Cleveland, Inc.
gratefully acknowledges
the generous support of

MASTER CHEF
Nestlé

SOUS CHEFS

CORPORATE

APCOA, Inc.

The Cleveland Clinic
Foundation

Cleveland Menu Printing

The Huntington
National Bank

Ideal Macaroni Company

Kenny King Corporation

The Perlmuter Printing
Company

Smythe, Cramer Company

Squire, Sanders & Dempsey

INDIVIDUAL

Mr. & Mrs. Arthur J.
Althans II

Susan & Greg Althans

Margie & Jim Biggar

Bonnie Femec

Helen & Geof Greenleaf

Carol Holder

Cathleen Lane

Joyce Litzler

Lisa Mullin

Patty & Broock Munro

Georgia Stonehill

Julia Sullivan

CHEFS DE CUISINE

Debbie & Richard Bedell
Deborah & David Corbets
Bonnie & Lewis Femec
Belinda & David Fouts
Betsy & Michael Grodhaus
Debbie & Bob Hermann
Carol Holder
Sarah Lane
Carol B. & Donald Lewellen
Joyce Litzler
Carolyn & Jim Newman

Sylvia Oliver
Patti & David Paddock
Vanessa & Christopher Pasiadis
Virginia E. Paterson
Kathy Pender
Beth Petrequin & David Young
Mary Lou DeGrandis Slife
Lee Anne & Gerald Stueber
Ginny & John Wilhelm
Adrienne & Cliff Wilson
Patricia Motch

Corporate Sponsor
KFC

THE CLEVELAND CLINIC FOUNDATION

As a guide for those readers and cooks who seek delicious but health-wise recipes, throughout **A Cleveland Collection** the reader will find The Cleveland Clinic Foundation logo as a symbol indicating that a recipe is considered within The Cleveland Clinic Foundation's guidelines for healthy eating. This means that when prepared in the notated serving size that the first course recipes have no more than 150 calories, 6 grams of fat and 450 milligrams of sodium per serving; main dish recipes have no more than 300 calories, 11 grams of fat and 700 milligrams of sodium per serving; side dish recipes have no more than 100 calories, 2.5 grams of fat and 250 milligrams of sodium; dessert recipes have no more than 150 calories, 4.5 grams of fat and 100 milligrams of sodium.

An evening in the Flats

When the sun sets and the lights shimmer, it is time for a grand performance. It is time to whet the appetite, pique the curiosity and enchant your family and friends with a very special appetizer. Inspired by a symphony of flavors these enticing recipes should bring splendid harmony to all occasions.

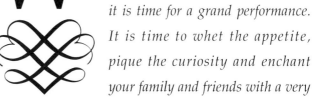

Player's Pizza and Pasta Restaurant

ROASTED GARLIC

4   heads garlic, some outer paper
    removed
    Olive oil

❖ *P*reheat oven to 350 degrees.
Coat the garlic heads with olive oil. Wrap in
a double layer of aluminum foil. Bake at 350
degrees for 30 to 45 minutes. Cool. Serve
with thinly sliced French bread or melba
toast.

using less than 6 tbls oil

TOMATO and BASIL
CROUSTADES

Yield: 14-16 slices

3   plum tomatoes, chopped
1/4 cup pine nuts
3   tablespoons olive oil
3   tablespoons fresh basil, chopped
1   teaspoon dried oregano
1   baguette French bread, sliced

❖ *C*ombine tomatoes, pine nuts,
olive oil, basil and oregano. Refrigerate for
2-3 hours. Toast baguette slices and top with
marinated tomato mixture.

*This page has been underwritten through
the generosity of* HELEN & GEOF GREENLEAF.

GREEN PEPPERCORN DIP

Yield: 3 cups

1	(8-oz.) pkg. cream cheese, softened
2/3	cup sour cream
2/3	cup mayonnaise
1/4	cup minced green onion
2-4	tablespoons chopped fresh parsley
1/4	cup bottled green peppercorns, drained
2	tablespoons fresh lemon juice
1	teaspoon paprika
1-2	dashes Tabasco sauce (optional)
1/2	cup finely chopped celery

❖ Combine cream cheese, sour cream, mayonnaise, onion, parsley, peppercorns, lemon juice, paprika and Tabasco sauce in food processor; process until smooth. Stir in celery. Place in medium bowl. Cover and refrigerate several hours. Serve with vegetable crudites.

HUMMUS DIP with FRESH PITA CHIPS

Servings: 8-10

Hummus

4	cloves garlic, minced
2	cups chick peas, cooked and drained
1/4	cup lemon juice
1/4	cup Tahini (sesame paste)
1	tablespoon soy sauce
1/4	cup water
	Tabasco sauce
	Salt and pepper

Pita Chips

Pita rounds
Melted butter
Olive oil
Seasoned salt
Dried thyme

❖ HUMMUS: Combine garlic, chick peas, lemon juice, Tahini and soy sauce in blender or food processor; process until smooth. Add water and blend until lighter consistency. Season with Tabasco, salt and pepper to taste.

PITA CHIPS: Preheat oven to 250 degrees. Cut each pita into 6 triangles; open pieces and brush with olive oil and butter; lightly sprinkle with seasoned salt or dried thyme. Bake at 250 degrees on cookie sheet for 30 minutes or until crisp.

OLIVE CROSTINI

Servings: 8

1   cup pitted Calamata olives

2   tablespoons virgin olive oil or walnut oil

4-5   cloves garlic, crushed

      Anchovy paste (2" squeeze from tube)

1/4   cup freshly grated Parmesan cheese

1   baguette French bread, sliced 1/2-inch thick

1/2   cup Mozzarella cheese

❖ *P*reheat oven to 325 degrees. Combine olives, oil, garlic, anchovy paste and Parmesan cheese in food processor until well blended; scrape down sides of bowl frequently. Spread mixture on bread slices; top with pinch of Mozzarella cheese. Place on cookie sheet and bake at 325 degrees for 10 minutes or until cheese is melted. Serve immediately.

BAKED ASPARAGUS APPETIZER

Servings: 16

30   fresh asparagus spears, cleaned and trimmed

1/2   cup mayonnaise

1   tablespoon all-purpose flour

1   cup grated Mozzarella cheese

1   cup grated Cheddar cheese

1/2   teaspoon prepared mustard

      Salt and pepper to taste

1/2   teaspoon lemon zest

2   sheets frozen puff pastry, thawed

1   egg, beaten

❖ *S*team asparagus just until tender. Cut 20 asparagus spears into 1-inch logs. Mash remaining spears. In small bowl, combine mashed asparagus, mayonnaise, flour, Mozzarella cheese, Cheddar cheese, mustard, salt, pepper and lemon zest. Roll puff pastry sheets into 17-inch squares. Place 1/2 of mixture on each square; top each with 1/2 of asparagus logs. Fold pastry in half and seal edges. Brush dough with beaten egg. Bake at 375 degrees for 15 to 20 minutes or until puffed and golden. Cut into strips to serve.

VARIATION: Serve for brunch or luncheon, pass a light hollandaise sauce on the side.

LAYERED TORTE in HOLLOWED-OUT BREAD

Servings: 8

2 cloves garlic, minced

4 tablespoons butter

2 (10-oz.) pkgs. chopped spinach, thawed and squeezed dry

1/2 cup plus 2 tablespoons freshly grated Parmesan cheese

Freshly ground pepper

1 red bell pepper, cut into 1 x 1/2-inch strips

1 round loaf Italian bread (6 1/2-inch diameter)

8 oz. sliced Swiss cheese

4 oz. thinly sliced proscuito ham

Olive oil

❖ *P*reheat oven to 350 degrees. Saute garlic over low heat in 2 tablespoons butter for 1 minute. Add spinach, Parmesan cheese and remaining butter. Saute until cheese is melted. Cool; season with freshly ground pepper. Cover red pepper with water in small saucepan; simmer until pepper is soft. Drain and pat dry. Slice off top of bread 1 1/2-inches from top. Hollow out bread leaving 1/4-inch sides. Line bottom and sides of bread cavity with slices of Swiss cheese. Divide remaining Swiss cheese into 3 parts. Spread bottom of bread with 1/2 of spinach mixture. Top with a layer of Swiss cheese. Arrange 1/2 of ham over cheese layer. Arrange peppers over top of ham; top with remaining ham. Top with a layer of Swiss cheese. Spread remaining spinach mixture over top and cover with remaining cheese. Place bread "lid" over top. Brush entire loaf liberally with olive oil. Wrap tightly in foil. Bake at 350 degrees for 25 minutes. Refrigerate until torte is thoroughly cooled. Serve cold or tepid.

ARTICHOKE DIP

Servings: 8

1   (8-oz.) can artichoke hearts,
    drained and chopped
1   cup grated sharp Cheddar cheese
1   cup grated Parmesan cheese
1/2 cup mayonnaise
1/2 cup chopped green onions
1-2 cloves garlic, minced

❖ *P*reheat oven to 350 degrees.
Combine all ingredients; mix well. Pour into
oven-proof serving dish. Bake at 350 degrees
for 20 minutes or until bubbly. Serve with
pita chips or assorted crackers.

VARIATIONS: Add 1/4 cup
slivered almonds; spread on toasted party
rye. Bake at 350 degrees until bubbly.

CHUTNEY GLAZED
HEARTS of PALM

Servings: 24-30

1   (8 1/2-oz.) can hearts of palm,
    drained
1   (12-oz.) pkg. bacon slices,
    partially cooked, cut in half
1   (9-oz.) jar chutney

❖ *P*reheat oven to 350 degrees.
Cut hearts of palm into 1 1/2-inch long
pieces. Wrap each with bacon and secure
with toothpicks. Place on cookie sheet.
Spread with chutney. Bake at 350 degrees
until bacon is fully cooked and well glazed.

MINTED HERB BAGUETTES

Yield: 12-14 slices

2/3 cup mayonnaise

1/3 cup sour cream

1/4 cup finely chopped scallions

1/4 cup finely chopped fresh mint

1 baguette French bread, sliced

❖ Combine mayonnaise, sour cream, scallions and mint. Refrigerate 2 to 3 hours. Spread mixture onto bread slices. Serve chilled.

CELERY STUFFED with GORGONZOLA and GOAT CHEESE

Servings: 6-8

3-4 stalks celery

1/4 lb. Gorgonzola cheese

1/4 lb. Montrachet or other mild goat cheese

2 tablespoons heavy cream

1/4 cup chopped walnuts

❖ Slice each celery stalk into 4 pieces. Combine cheeses and cream. Place cheese mixture in pastry bag fitted with star tip. Pipe cheese mixture into each piece of celery. Sprinkle with nuts.

VARIATION: Substitute herbed goat cheese for Montrachet; endive for celery.

PESTO and GOAT CHEESE CROSTINI

Yield: 10-15

Pesto

- 2 cups fresh basil leaves
- 2 cloves garlic
- 1/2 cup plus 2 tablespoons Parmesan cheese
- 2 tablespoons pine nuts
- 1/2 teaspoon salt
- 1/2 cup extra virgin olive oil

- 1 loaf French bread
- 3/4 cup chopped Calamata black olives
- 3/4 cup sundried tomatoes, drained (type soaked in olive oil, garlic and basil)
- 8 oz. goat cheese, crumbled

❖ *P*ESTO: Place basil and garlic in food processor; process until mixture is pureed. Add Parmesan cheese, pine nuts and salt; continue to process until smooth. With processor running, slowly add oil and process until well combined. If a thinner pesto is desired, add additional oil.

Slice bread into 1/2-inch slices. Using basting brush, spread pesto on each slice. Sprinkle, in order, sundried tomatoes, olives and goat cheese. Broil 4 to 6 inches from heat for 3 to 4 minutes or until pesto starts to bubble and cheese is melted.

CHEVRE PESTO PATÉ

Servings: 8

- 3 tablespoons chopped hazelnuts
- 8 oz. cream-style Chevre cheese, softened
- 4 oz. cream cheese, softened
- 1 1/2 cups fresh basil leaves, lightly packed
- 1/3 cup grated Romano cheese
- 2 tablespoons olive oil
- 2 tablespoons unsalted butter, softened
- Oil

❖ *I*n a deep bowl, using hand-held blender, combine chevre and cream cheese until smooth but not liquid. In another deep bowl, using hand-held blender, puree basil leaves, Romano cheese and olive oil; add nuts and butter; using whisk attachment whisk mixture for a few seconds. Oil a 7 x 4 x 2 1/4-inch loaf pan; line with wax paper and brush lightly with oil. Spread 1/2 of cheese mixture into pan; smooth surface. Cover with pesto sauce. Top with remaining cheese mixture; cover pan. Refrigerate several hours or overnight.

To serve, invert pan onto serving plate. Gently remove pan and wax paper. Garnish with basil leaves and hazelnuts. Serve with wheat crackers.

PATÉ PAS RAFFINE

Servings: 6-12

1 **lb. poultry livers (duck, chicken, goose or turkey)**

1 **apple, cut into 1/4-inch cubes**

10 **tablespoons unsalted butter**

3 **tablespoons Calvados apple brandy**

1 **tablespoon finely minced onions**

2 **tablespoons finely minced shallots**

   Salt

   Pepper

   Pinch of allspice

1/2 **cup whipping cream**

1 **tablespoon sour cream**

1/4 **cup clarified butter**

❖ *C*lean poultry livers of all membranes. Saute apple cubes in 2 table-spoons butter over high heat (apples will turn light brown very fast). Quickly stir in 1 tablespoon Calvados. Transfer apples and Calvados to small bowl. Add 2 tablespoons butter to pan. Heat until butter turns medium brown. Add onions; saute 2 minutes. Add shallots and livers. Saute over high heat until livers turn uniformly gray outside but remain rare inside. Add salt, pepper and allspice. Add remaining 2 tablespoons Calvados and ignite; allow flame to die. Remove from heat. Mash all ingredients together with a fork while still hot to obtain a semi-liquid, rough puree. Strain through a wire strainer, pushing hard with a wooden spoon. Cool the mixture. In a large mixing bowl, cream 6 tablespoons butter. Gradually add liver mixture. Add apples and Calvados. Mix well. Beat whipping cream and sour cream until mixture mounds slightly. Fold into liver mixture. Pack paté in a 1/2-quart souffle dish or terrine. Cool and pour clarified butter over surface of paté to seal. Refrigerate 6 hours or overnight.

Along the lagoon in University Circle

CHEESE and PESTO TORTA with PINE NUTS

Servings: 8

Pesto

3	tablespoons olive oil
1	medium clove garlic
1	cup basil leaves, stems trimmed
1/2	cup pine nuts, lightly toasted
1/2	teaspoon black pepper
1/8	teaspoon cayenne pepper
1/2	cup Parmesan cheese, freshly grated

Cheese

1/4	cup unsalted butter, softened
4	oz. cream cheese, softened
6	oz. fresh goat cheese

❖ *P*ESTO: In a food processor or blender, puree olive oil and garlic; add basil and continue to puree. Add 1/4 cup pine nuts and puree. Add black pepper, cayenne pepper and Parmesan cheese; process until mixture forms a thick paste. Mixture should be spreadable; if too thick add oil a few drops at a time.

CHEESE: In small bowl, beat butter, cream cheese and goat cheese until smooth. Line a 2-cup mold or bowl with plastic wrap. Spoon in 1/2 of the cheese mixture; arrange 1/4 cup pine nuts over the cheese; spoon the pesto over the nuts. Smooth top to make an even layer. Top with remaining cheese mixture (pesto may color the cheese a bit); cover and chill. To serve, unmold on a plate; carefully remove plastic wrap. Garnish with fresh basil leaves. Serve with warm crusty Italian or sourdough bread.

HOT CHEDDAR BITES

Servings: 12

6   English muffins, split
1   cup chopped black olives
1 1/2   cups grated sharp white Cheddar cheese
1/2   cup finely chopped onion
1/2   cup mayonnaise
1/2   teaspoon curry powder
1/2   teaspoon salt

❖ *P*reheat broiler. In medium bowl, combine all ingredients except muffins. Spread each muffin half with 2 tablespoons of mixture. Place muffins on cookie sheet and broil until cheese is melted and light brown. Cool slightly; cut into quarters. Serve warm.

SAVORY MUSHROOM PALMIERS

Yield: 60 pieces

5   tablespoons unsalted butter
1   lb. fresh mushrooms, finely chopped
1   medium onion, minced
3/4   teaspoon lemon juice
2   tablespoons all-purpose flour
1 1/2   teaspoons dried thyme, crushed
    Salt and pepper, to taste
3   frozen puff pastry sheets, thawed
2   eggs
4   teaspoons half-and-half or water

❖ *S*aute mushrooms and onion in butter until juice is evaporated, stirring occasionally. Blend in lemon juice, flour and thyme; season with salt and pepper. Cook for 2 minutes; remove from heat and cool completely. Unfold puff pastry and roll to smooth creases. Spread 1/3 of the mushroom mixture on each sheet. Starting at one long end, roll up the pastry stopping at center. Repeat from the opposite side. Cover and refrigerate until well chilled.

Preheat oven to 400 degrees. In small bowl, beat together eggs and cream. Using a sharp serrated knife, slice each pastry roll into 1/4-inch slices. Arrange 1-inch apart on ungreased cookie sheets. Brush with beaten egg mixture. Bake 15 to 20 minutes or until golden and puffed.

VARIATION: Add 1 tablespoon Madeira wine and substitute 1 tablespoon chopped chives for the thyme and wild mushrooms for domestic.

MARINATED MUSHROOMS

Yield: 1 3/4 cups

2/3   cup vegetable oil

1/2   cup vinegar

1   (0.7-oz.) pkg. Italian dressing mix

1   tablespoon lemon juice

1   teaspoon dried basil leaves, crushed

12   oz. fresh mushrooms

2   tablespoons chopped parsley

2   tablespoons chopped pimento (optional)

❖ *I*n large saucepan, combine oil, vinegar, dressing mix, lemon juice and basil. Heat to boiling. Add mushrooms. Simmer 3 minutes, stirring constantly. Add parsley and pimento. Refrigerate for 6 hours or overnight.

MUSHROOM PINROLLS

Servings: 8

1   large onion, finely chopped

1   tablespoon butter

12   oz. mushrooms, finely chopped

1/4   teaspoon salt

1/8   teaspoon pepper

12   oz. cream cheese, softened

1/2   teaspoon Worcestershire sauce

1/4   teaspoon garlic powder

1   loaf thinly sliced sandwich bread

2   tablespoons butter, softened

❖ *S*aute onions in butter until golden. Add mushrooms and saute for 2 minutes. Remove from heat. Season with salt and pepper. Add cream cheese and blend until smooth. Stir in Worcestershire sauce and garlic powder. Remove crusts from bread; cut each slice in half. Roll each slice flat and spread 1/2 teaspoon mushroom mixture on each. Roll lengthwise, jelly roll fashion; cut in half. Can be frozen at this point; defrost before heating. Preheat broiler. Spread butter lightly on each pinroll. Place on cookie sheet and broil until brown and bubbly. Serve immediately.

FRESH PORCINI MUSHROOMS BAKED with BACON

Servings: 8

8   very large fresh porcini mush-
    rooms, cleaned, trimmed and
    halved
    Olive oil
16 slices thick-cut lean bacon
    Freshly ground black pepper
    Cilantro

❖ *P*reheat oven to 450 degrees.
Generously brush mushroom halves on all
sides with olive oil. Wrap each in bacon and
place on baking sheet. Bake at 450 degrees
about 8 to 10 minutes or until bacon is crisp.
Remove to warm serving plates and top with
generous amount of black pepper. Garnish
with cilantro.

ENDIVE with WILD MUSHROOMS and PARSLEY

Yield: 40 Appetizers

1   lb. fresh wild mushrooms
    (chanterells, pleurottes, shitake,
    porcini), cut into 1/2-inch pieces
6   tablespoons olive oil
    Salt
    Freshly ground pepper
6   tablespoons chopped fresh parsley
1/2 cup whipping cream
40 small endive leaves

❖ *S*aute mushrooms in olive oil for
2 to 3 minutes. Season with salt and pepper.
Add parsley and cream and bring to a simmer. Remove from heat. Spoon onto endive
leaves and serve immediately.

SAVORY PARTY RYE

Servings: 8

1 lb. pork sausage
1 lb. lean ground beef
2 small onions, grated
1 tablespoon dried oregano
1/2 teaspoon garlic powder
1/2 teaspoon Worcestershire sauce
1 lb. grated Mozzarella cheese
1 (8-oz.) loaf cocktail rye bread

❖ *H*eat oven to 350 degrees. In large skillet, brown sausage and beef; drain. Add onions, oregano, garlic powder and Worcestershire sauce. Cook until onions are soft. Add grated cheese; stir until melted. Remove from heat. Spread mixture on bread rounds. Place on baking sheet. Bake at 350 degrees for 12 to 15 minutes. Sprinkle with parsley for color. Can be prepared ahead. Appetizers can be frozen before baking.

VARIATION: Substitute 1 lb. sharp Cheddar cheese for Mozzarella; 1 lb. turkey sausage for pork sausage.

SOUTH of the BORDER SPINACH DIP

Servings: 8-10

1 (4-oz.) can chopped green chilies, drained
3/4 cup chopped onion
2 tomatoes, chopped
2 teaspoons chopped cilantro
1 (10-oz.) pkg. frozen spinach, thawed and squeezed dry
1 (8-oz.) pkg. cream cheese, softened
2 cups shredded Monterey Jack cheese
1/3 cup half-and-half
1-2 dashes Tabasco sauce

❖ *P*reheat oven to 400 degrees. Butter a 1-qt. baking dish. Combine all ingredients. Pour into prepared pan. Bake at 400 degrees for 20 to 25 minutes. Serve with tortilla chips or toasted pita bread.

PROSCIUTTO with LEMON and DILL

Yield: 24

24   thin slices prosciutto ham

2   tablespoons minced fresh dill

2   teaspoons minced lemon peel

3   medium limes, cut into thin wedges

❖ *R*oll the prosciutto into a trumpet or cylinder shape. Combine the dill and lemon peel. Sprinkle over prosciutto. Serve with lime wedges.

GLAZED BACON

Yield: 40 pieces

1   lb. bacon

1-2   cups firmly packed brown sugar

❖ *P*reheat oven to 300 degrees. Pat a thin layer of brown sugar on bottom of cookie sheet or jelly roll pan. Cut bacon slices in half; place bacon slices close together on top of sugar. Generously sprinkle brown sugar over top of bacon. Bake at 300 degrees for 10 minutes. Turn bacon. Bake for additional 10 minutes or until bacon is cooked through. Remove from oven. Drain on paper towel. Serve at room temperature; garnish with fresh parsley.

SMOKED TURKEY CANAPES

Yield: 40 canapes

1/2 cup Dijon mustard
2 tablespoons honey
1 loaf thinly sliced bread
2 lbs. thinly sliced smoked turkey breast
Boston lettuce

❖ Combine mustard and honey. Spread on bread slices. Top half of bread slices with turkey and lettuce leaf. Top with remaining bread to make sandwich. Cut sandwiches into quarters and arrange on serving platter. Cover tightly with foil and refrigerate. Can be made up to 8 hours before serving.

LAMB and PASTRY CANAPES

Yield: 24 canapes

2 teaspoons butter
1 tablespoon oil
1 small onion, minced
8 oz. ground lamb
1/2 teaspoon cumin
1/2 teaspoon rosemary
1 clove garlic
1/2 teaspoon ground cloves
1-2 teaspoons cornstarch
2 tablespoons water
2 tablespoons apricot nectar
1 1/2 tablespoons mint jelly
1 – 2 sheets frozen puff pastry, thawed

❖ In large skillet, heat butter and oil. Add onions; saute over medium heat until transparent. Add lamb. Cook over low heat until browned; drain. Return pan to low heat. Add cumin, rosemary, garlic and cloves. Simmer 15 minutes. In small bowl, combine cornstarch, water and apricot nectar. Add mixture to skillet. Stir until meat mixture is well coated. Simmer 2 minutes. Add jelly; cool. Cut dough into 48 squares. Place 1 teaspoon of lamb mixture in center of 24 squares. Cover with remaining squares. Seal edges with fork. Bake at 375 degrees for 8 to 12 minutes. Serve immediately.

SWEET and SOUR MEATBALLS

Yield: 50-60 appetizers

Sauce

1	cup firmly packed brown sugar
1	teaspoon dry mustard
1/2	cup vinegar
1/2	cup water

Meatballs

1	lb. ground ham
1 1/2	lb. ground pork
1 1/4	cups bread crumbs
2	eggs, beaten
1	cup milk

❖ *S*AUCE: Preheat oven to 325 degrees. Combine brown sugar, mustard, vinegar and water until sugar is dissolved.

MEATBALLS: In large bowl, mix ham, pork, bread crumbs, eggs and milk until well combined. Roll meat mixture into balls approximately 1-inch in diameter. Place close together in a 9 x 13-inch pan. Cover with sauce. Bake at 325 degrees for 60 minutes, basting occasionally.

MASSIMO DA MILANO

VEAL and SAGE MEATBALLS

Yield: 50-60 appetizers

1 1/2	lb. ground veal
1/4	cup chopped fresh sage
3	tablespoons half-and-half
1/3	cup grated Parmesan cheese
3	tablespoons minced garlic
1/2	teaspoon salt
1/2	teaspoon pepper
1	cup bread crumbs
2	eggs, beaten
1/3	cup chopped fresh parsley

❖ *P*reheat oven to 350 degrees. In large bowl, combine all ingredients. Roll meat mixture into balls approximately 1-inch in diameter. Place on baking sheets. Bake at 350 degrees for 30 minutes.

GREEK MEATBALLS

Yield: 25-35 meatballs

Meatballs

1 1/2 lbs. ground round steak

2 slices white bread, soaked in water, squeezed dry

1 egg

1 medium onion, chopped

1/2 cup chopped parsley

1/2 teaspoon dried mint, crushed

1/2 teaspoon salt

1/4 teaspoon pepper

2 teaspoons ground cumin

Flour

Olive oil

Vegetable oil

Tomato Sauce

1 (16-oz.) can pureed tomatoes

1 (15-oz.) can tomato sauce

2–3 tablespoons red wine

1/2 teaspoon cinnamon

1 bay leaf

Salt and pepper to taste

1 teaspoon sugar

1/2 cup water

❖ MEATBALLS: In large bowl, combine beef, bread, egg, onion, parsley, mint, salt, pepper, and cumin. If mixture seems dry, add small amount of water to moisten. Roll meat mixture into small balls approximately 1 1/2 to 2 inches in diameter. Roll meatballs in flour. In large skillet over medium heat, saute meatballs in equal parts olive and vegetable oil. Turn meatballs to cook on all sides. Drain.

TOMATO SAUCE: Combine all ingredients. Place meatballs in baking dish. Pour sauce over meatballs. Bake at 250 degrees for 2 hours.

STUFFED GRAPE LEAVES with EGG LEMON SAUCE

Yield: 50-60

Stuffed Grape Leaves

1	(16-oz.) jar grape leaves
1 1/2	lbs. lean ground beef
1/2	cup long grain rice
3	large onions, minced
	Salt and pepper
1/2	tablespoon minced fresh mint
1/2	tablespoon dill
1/2	cup water
3	tablespoons olive oil
1 1/2	tablespoons tomato paste
1	(16-oz.) can peeled, crushed tomatoes

Egg-Lemon Sauce

1/2	cup plain yogurt
1	cup reserved cooking juices
1 1/4	tablespoons cornstarch
2	tablespoons cold water
4	eggs, beaten
5	tablespoons lemon juice
	Dash of white pepper
	Dash of salt

❖ *S*TUFFED GRAPE LEAVES: Drain brine from grape leaves. Snip off stems and rinse under cold running water; drain. Parboil leaves until tender; drain. In large bowl, combine ground beef, rice, onions, salt, pepper, mint, dill and water. Grease a Dutch oven. Spread any torn leaves on the bottom of dutch oven. With stem facing up, place 1 teaspoon of meat mixture on the base of the leaf. Fold sides over and roll up. Do not roll too tightly; the rice expands during cooking. Layer in circular fashion in Dutch oven seam side down. Shape any remaining meat mixture into meatballs and place on top. Add tomato paste, tomatoes and enough water to cover. Place an inverted, heavy plate on top of grape leaves to prevent shifting. Bring to a boil, reduce heat and simmer covered for 1 to 1 1/2 hours. Reserve cooking juices. Place in large serving dish; serve Egg-Lemon Sauce for dipping. Garnish with tomato segments from Dutch oven for color.

EGG-LEMON SAUCE: In medium bowl, combine yogurt and cooking broth; set aside. In medium saucepan, dissolve cornstarch in water, add eggs and beat well. Add lemon juice, salt and pepper. Beat well. Fold in yogurt mixture. Cook over low heat, beating constantly, until sauce thickens to consistency of whipping cream.

CRAB CURRY DIP

Yield: 2 cups

1   (6 ½-oz.) can lump crab meat
1   (8-oz.) pkg. cream cheese, softened
2   tablespoons chutney
1   teaspoon curry powder
2   tablespoons grated onion
¼   cup mayonnaise
    Dash pepper
¼   cup toasted slivered almonds

❖ *P*reheat oven to 350 degrees. Combine crab meat, cream cheese, chutney, curry powder, onion, mayonnaise and pepper until well blended. Place in oven proof serving dish; sprinkle with almonds. Bake at 350 degrees for 15 minutes or until lightly browned. Serve with assorted crackers.

VARIATION: Substitute 2 cups cooked chicken for crab. Process mixture in food processor 5 to 10 seconds or until well blended.

TARAMOSALATA

Servings: 12-15

2-3   medium size potatoes, boiled and peeled
2   (4 to 6-oz.) jars red fish roe (Tarama) or caviar
1   cup olive oil
    Juice of 1 ½ lemons
2   tablespoons vinegar
2   tablespoons water
1   small onion, grated
    Black olives
    Capers
    Chopped parsley

❖ *B*eat potatoes and fish roe at medium speed until smooth. Gradually add olive oil, lemon juice, vinegar and water. Beat until mixture is creamy and fluffy. Add onion; blend well. To serve, place in glass serving dish. Garnish with black olives, capers and parsley. Serve with water crackers such as Bremner or Carr.

CRAB STRUDEL

Servings: 15

1/2   lb. crabmeat

1   tablespoon lemon juice

1   tablespoon butter

2   tablespoons minced green onions

2   tablespoons parsley, chopped

2   drops Tabasco sauce

    Dash salt

    Dash pepper

1/2   lb. Brie cheese, cut into small, thin pieces

6   sheets frozen phyllo dough, thawed

2   tablespoons of melted butter

❖ *P*reheat oven to 375 degrees. Sprinkle lemon juice over crabmeat. Saute green onions in 1 tablespoon butter. Add crabmeat and heat through. Add parsley, Tabasco sauce, salt and pepper. Mix well. Place Brie slices over top of crabmeat mixture; allow to melt. Gently mix together. Stack 2 sheets of phyllo dough; brush with melted butter. Spread 1/3 of crab mixture along short end. Roll, tucking ends under; brush with butter. Place on cookie sheet. Repeat for remaining dough. Bake at 375 degrees for 20 to 25 minutes. To serve, slice each roll into 12 pieces.

VARIATION: Use Feta cheese and spinach in place of Brie and crab.

MAGNIFICENT MUSSELS

Servings: 10-12

10-12   shallots or green onions, chopped

2   cups dry white wine

1   medium onion, cut into eighths

5   lbs. mussels, scrubbed and debearded

Topping

8   cloves garlic

1/2   cup fresh parsley

1/4   cup white wine

1/2   cup olive oil

1/4   cup lemon juice

❖ *M*USSELS: Combine wine, shallots and onion in large saucepan; bring to a boil. Steam mussels for 5 to 8 minutes. Do not overcook. Drain. Remove top mussel shell. Place on large platter.

TOPPING: Combine all topping ingredients in food processor or blender. Process until well blended. Spoon over mussels. Cover with damp cloth and refrigerate until served.

SHRIMP PASTRIES

Yield: 32 appetizers

2 tablespoons unsalted butter

2 tablespoons minced onions or shallots

2 tablespoons all-purpose flour

1 cup half-and-half

2 tablespoons dry sherry

1/2 teaspoon lemon juice

1-2 drops Tabasco sauce

5 oz. baby shrimp

1 green onion, cut into fine julienne strips

3/4 cup finely grated Gruyere cheese

1 (17 1/4-oz.) pkg. frozen puff pastry sheets

1 egg, beaten

Paprika

Salt

White pepper

❖ *S*aute onions in butter until tender. Stir in flour and cook for 1 minute, stirring constantly. Whisk in half-and-half, sherry, lemon juice and Tabasco sauce. Cook, stirring until mixture thickens. Remove from heat and allow to cool completely. Season to taste with salt and pepper; add baby shrimp. Thaw puff pastry at room temperature for 20 minutes. On a lightly floured surface, roll each sheet into a 12-inch square. Cut into 16 3-inch squares. Top each square with a spoonful of the shrimp mixture; sprinkle green onion and cheese over each square. Brush edges of each square with egg. Fold pastry square in half to form a triangle. Press edges together with fork; brush top with egg. Dust with paprika. Transfer to ungreased cookie sheet. Bake at 400 degrees for 10 to 12 minutes or until puffed and golden.

CZAR'S CAVIAR SPREAD

Yield: 12 servings

8   large hard boiled eggs, peeled and chopped

2-3   tablespoons mayonnaise
    Freshly ground pepper

1   small onion, grated

1   (4-oz.) jar caviar, drained

1/2   cup sour cream
    Fresh chives, chopped
    Party rye bread rounds

❖ Combine eggs and mayonnaise; blend well. Season with pepper. Spread mixture in shallow serving dish. Carefully spread caviar over egg mixture. Stir sour cream; spread on top of caviar. Use more sour cream if needed to completely cover. Sprinkle with chives. Refrigerate. Serve with party rye or pumpernickel bread.

This page has been underwritten through the generosity of LISA MULLIN.

HYDE PARK GRILL

HOT CRAB SPREAD with GARLIC TOAST

Servings: 6

1   (8-oz.) pkg. cream cheese, softened

1   tablespoon milk

2   teaspoons Worcestershire sauce

8   oz. king crabmeat, flaked

2   tablespoons diced green onion

2   tablespoons slivered almonds, toasted
    Garlic toast

❖ Preheat oven to 350 degrees. Combine cream cheese, milk, Worcestershire sauce, crabmeat and green onions. Toss thoroughly. Place in small individual casseroles; sprinkle with almonds. Bake uncovered at 350 degrees for 15 minutes. Serve with garlic toast or assorted crackers.

SEAFOOD STRUDEL

Serves: 6-8

White Sauce

2	tablespoons butter
2	tablespoons all-purpose flour
1/2	teaspoon Dijon mustard
1/4	teaspoon dry mustard
	Salt
	Cayenne pepper
3/4	cup milk

Seafood

1	lb. seafood (crab, lobster, shrimp or combination)
1/2	cup grated Swiss cheese
2	hard boiled eggs, chopped
1/2	cup water chestnuts, chopped
3/4	cup sour cream
1/2	cup green onions
1/4	cup parsley, chopped
1	teaspoon minced garlic
1/2	cup butter, melted
2	tablespoons chopped parsley
2	tablespoons grated Parmesan cheese
4	sheets Phyllo dough

❖ WHITE SAUCE: Melt 2 tablespoons butter in medium saucepan. Stir in flour, Dijon mustard, dry mustard, salt and cayenne pepper; cook until mixture is smooth and bubbly. Gradually add milk.

Cook until mixture boils and thickens, stirring constantly. Remove from heat; chill until firm, about 2 hours.

SEAFOOD: Preheat oven to 375 degrees. Lightly oil a cookie sheet. Stack 2 phyllo sheets on waxed paper; brush with melted butter. (Keep remaining sheets of phyllo dough covered with damp towel.) Repeat, stacking 2 more layers. Place seafood on prepared phyllo dough. Top with Swiss cheese, hard boiled eggs and water chestnuts; dot with sour cream. Sprinkle green onions, parsley and garlic over top. Dot with chilled white sauce. Roll into strudel shape, tucking ends under. Place on prepared cookie sheet and brush with melted butter. Bake at 375 degrees for 12 minutes. Remove from oven, brush with butter and slice diagonally into 1 1/2-inch pieces. Return to oven and bake 35 to 40 minutes or until golden brown. Transfer to warm platter; brush with melted butter. Sprinkle parsley and 2 tablespoons Parmesan cheese over top.

VEGETABLE BLINI
with
SMOKED SALMON

Serves: 4-6

3   parsnips, peeled and grated

1/4   tart apple, grated

1/4   small onion, grated

1/3   cup all-purpose flour

2   eggs, lightly beaten

1   teaspoon salt

1/4   teaspoon ground pepper

2   tablespoons butter

1/4   cup oil

1/4   lb. smoked salmon

     Sour cream

     Fresh dill or chives

❖ *I*n large bowl, combine parsnips, apple and onion. Sprinkle with flour; toss to combine. Add eggs, salt and pepper; toss to combine. In large skillet, heat butter and oil. Using 1/2 tablespoon of vegetable mixture, form little pancakes. Flatten with back of spoon to make irregularly shaped 2-inch rounds. Brown on both sides, adding more butter and oil if necessary. Drain well on paper towel. Can be made ahead and frozen at this point. To reheat, place on baking sheets and heat at 400 degrees until crisp.

     Cut salmon into 1-inch by 1/4-inch strips. Top each pancake with 1/2 teaspoon sour cream. Lay 2 strips of salmon in cross over sour cream and sprinkle with dill or chives.

BACON and CHEESE
PARTY APPETIZERS

Yield: 24 appetizers

1   cup grated Swiss cheese

1/4   cup cooked bacon, crumbled

1   (4.5-oz.) can chopped ripe black olives

1/4   cup finely chopped green onions

1   teaspoon Worcestershire sauce

1/4   cup mayonnaise

1   (8-oz.) loaf cocktail rye bread

❖ *P*reheat oven to 350 degrees. Combine all ingredients except bread. Spread lightly on bread slices. Place on ungreased cookie sheet. Bake at 350 degrees approximately 10-15 minutes or until cheese melts.

FIESTA QUESADILLA

Yield: 24 appetizers

Olive oil

12 (6-inch diameter) flour tortillas

1½-2 cups grated cheese (combination of Monterey Jack, Colby, and Cheddar

1 yellow pepper, roasted and cut into strips

1 Anaheim or Poblano chile pepper, roasted and cut into strips

½ cup salsa

½ cup sour cream

Paprika

❖ *H*eat a cast iron skillet over low heat. Brush bottom of pan lightly with olive oil. Place a tortilla in pan. Sprinkle with 2 tablespoons of cheese. Cover with another tortilla and 2 tablespoons of cheese. Top with slices of roasted peppers. Cover and cook over low heat 5 to 7 minutes. Remove to cutting board and slice into quarters. Top with 1 tablespoon of salsa and a dollop of sour cream. If desired, dust with paprika. Repeat for remaining tortillas. Serve warm.

NOTE: To roast peppers, char over gas flame or under broiler until blackened all over. Place in paper bag for several minutes. Peel skin, remove seeds and stem.

MEXICAN CHIP DIP

Yield: 12 Servings

3 eggs, lightly beaten

2 (4-oz.) cans chopped green chili peppers, drained

4 cups grated Cheddar cheese

❖ *P*reheat oven to 350 degrees. Combine eggs, chili peppers and cheese. Pour into 1 ½ quart baking dish. Bake at 350 degrees for 30 to 60 minutes or until mixture is set. Serve with salsa and tortilla chips.

GRANNY APPLE CANAPE

Yield: 24 Servings

1   (8-oz.) loaf cocktail rye bread
1   Granny Smith apple, cored, peeled and minced
1   cup coarsely grated sharp Cheddar cheese
3   tablespoons mayonnaise
1½ tablespoons honey
1   teaspoon Dijon mustard
    Freshly ground pepper to taste

❖ *P*reheat broiler. Place bread on cookie sheet. Lightly toast under broiler. In small bowl, combine remaining ingredients. Mix well. If necessary, moisten with additional mayonnaise until spreading consistency. Spread mixture on bread. Broil until cheese is bubbly. Serve immediately.

JEZEBEL SPREAD

Yield: 48 Servings

1   (18-oz.) jar apple jelly
1   (18-oz.) jar pineapple preserves
1   (5-oz.) jar horseradish, drained
1   (1.5-oz.) can dry mustard
1   tablespoon cracked pepper
2   (8-oz.) pkgs. cream cheese
    Assorted crackers

❖ *C*ombine apple jelly, pineapple preserves, horseradish, dry mustard and cracked pepper in medium bowl. Mix well using wire whisk. Cover and refrigerate. To serve, place cream cheese on serving plates; generously spoon spread over the top. Serve with assorted crackers.

Soups & Salads

Severance Hall

What better way to capture summer's bounty or celebrate the warmth of good friends than with the alluring tastes of a tantalizing soup and salad. Embellish your menu with these pleasures or enjoy them as magical meals in themselves... while reading in the garden, sailing on the lake, enjoying the beach, or at home with family and close friends.

ROQUEFORT VICHYSSOISE

Servings: 8

- 2 cups finely chopped onion
- 1/4 cup butter or margarine
- 4 cups chicken broth
- 2 cups diced potatoes
- 1/4 teaspoon salt
- Pinch white pepper
- 4 oz. mild Roquefort cheese
- 1/2 cup dry white wine
- 2 cups buttermilk
- Chopped parsley
- Chopped chives
- Freshly cracked pepper

❖ *I*n large saucepan, saute onion in butter. Stir in broth, potatoes, salt and pepper. Bring to a boil. Reduce heat and simmer uncovered 15 minutes or until potatoes are tender. Puree in blender or food processor; return to pan. Stir in cheese and wine. Cook over low heat 5 minutes or until cheese melts. Cool and refrigerate covered 4 hours. Just before serving, stir in buttermilk. Garnish with parsley, chives and freshly cracked pepper.

MUSHROOM BRIE SOUP

Servings: 6-8

- 2 medium onions, chopped
- 1 clove garlic, crushed
- 4 tablespoons butter
- 12 oz. fresh mushrooms
- 1 1/4 teaspoons lemon juice
- 2 tablespoons all-purpose flour
- 4 cups chicken stock
- 1 cup light cream
- 1/2 cup whipping cream
- 2 oz. Brie, white rind removed, melted
- 1 tablespoon sherry
- Salt and pepper
- 2 oz. Brie, white rind removed, thinly sliced

❖ *S*aute onion and garlic in butter. Add mushrooms and lemon juice; cook 10 minutes. Add flour; cook 2 minutes. Chop mixture in blender or food processor; return to pan. Add chicken stock. Cook over low heat until slightly thickened. Add cream and melted Brie. Stir in sherry, salt and pepper to taste. Preheat broiler. Ladle soup into oven-proof bowls. Place thin slice of Brie on each serving. Broil soup until Brie is golden brown. Serve with crusty French bread.

ASPARAGUS and WILD RICE SOUP with TOASTED PECANS

Servings: 8

2³/₄ lbs. fresh asparagus
2 tablespoons butter
1 large onion, coarsely chopped
4 cups chicken stock
1 cup wild rice
1 tablespoons butter
¹/₂ cup chopped pecans
1 teaspoon sugar
   Pinch of salt
4 cups water
1 cup whipping cream
   Salt and freshly ground pepper
1 teaspoon fresh lemon juice

❖ Cut off top 2-inches of asparagus. Cut tops into ¹/₂-inch pieces; reserve. Coarsely chop remaining asparagus. In large saucepan, melt 2 tablespoons butter. Add onion and chopped asparagus; cook until onion is translucent. Stir in chicken stock and ¹/₂ cup wild rice. Bring to a boil. Reduce heat and simmer covered until rice is tender, about 1 hour.

In large saucepan, heat water to boiling. Add asparagus tips and cook until crisp tender, about 2 minutes. Remove tips with slotted spoon. Return water to a boil and add ¹/₂ cup rice. Simmer 45 minutes or until rice is tender. Drain.

Preheat oven to 350 degrees. Saute pecans, sugar and salt in 1 tablespoon butter for 1 minute. Transfer to baking sheet. Bake at 350 degrees for 8 minutes or until golden brown.

Puree soup in food processor or blender; return to saucepan. Stir in cream and rice. Season with salt and pepper. Add lemon juice, if desired. Garnish with asparagus tops and pecans.

This page has been underwritten through the generosity of CAROL HOLDER.

PUMPKIN SOUP

Servings: 8

6   cups chicken broth
2-3 cups cooked pumpkin
1   cup thinly sliced onion
1   clove garlic, minced
1½ teaspoons salt
½   teaspoon dried thyme
5   peppercorns
½   cup whipping cream, warmed
1   teaspoon chopped fresh parsley

❖ *I*n large saucepan, combine broth, pumpkin, onion, garlic, salt, thyme and peppercorns over medium-high heat. Bring to a boil; reduce heat. Uncover and simmer 40 minutes. Stir in cream. Garnish with parsley.

NOTE: This soup looks fantastic served in a hollowed-out pumpkin.

WINTER VEGETABLE and BARLEY CHOWDER

Servings: 6-8

½   cup pearl barley
1   cup water
3   tablespoons butter
1   cup diced cooked ham
1   large onion, chopped
3   cloves garlic, minced
1   medium carrot, peeled and diced
1   medium parsnip, peeled and diced
1   cup diced rutabaga
1   leek, rinsed well and chopped
1   cup finely shredded cabbage
6   cups chicken stock
1   cup whipping cream
    Salt and pepper
    Freshly grated nutmeg to taste

❖ *S*oak barley in water 6 hours or overnight. Drain. Melt butter in large saucepan; saute ham 5 minutes. Stir in onion; cook for 2 minutes. Add garlic; cook for 3 minutes. Stir in carrots, parsnips, rutabaga, leek and cabbage. Cook covered for 10 minutes. Add chicken broth. Bring to a boil; simmer 30 minutes. Stir in barley; simmer for 15 minutes. Reduce heat. Stir in cream. Season with salt, pepper and nutmeg to taste.

CREAM of POBLANO SOUP with CHEESE CRUST

Servings: 4

3 Poblano peppers, seeded, stems removed

1/2 cup diced onions

1/4 cup diced carrots

2 tablespoons butter

2 tablespoons all-purpose flour

4 cups chicken stock

2 tablespoons chopped fresh cilantro

3/4 cup whipping cream

Salt and pepper

12 tortilla chips

4 slices Monterey Jack cheese

❖ *S*aute peppers, onions and carrots in butter for 5 minutes. Reduce heat. Add flour and cook 5 minutes. Whisk in chicken stock and simmer 30 minutes. Remove from heat. Puree in blender or food processor. Return to pan. Add cilantro and cream. Season with salt and pepper to taste. Heat through. Preheat broiler. Ladle soup into oven-proof bowls. Top each bowl with 3 tortilla chips and slice of cheese. Place under broiler until cheese melts. Serve immediately.

ITALIAN SAUSAGE SOUP

Servings: 6-8

1/2 lb. sweet Italian sausage

1/2 lb. hot Italian sausage

2 cloves garlic, minced

1 cup chopped onion

2 carrots, peeled and diced

3/4 lb. zucchini, diced

1 green pepper, diced

1/2 cup white wine

5 cups chicken broth

1 lb. fresh or canned Italian plum tomatoes, peeled and chopped

2 teaspoons dried basil

1 teaspoon dried oregano

Freshly ground black pepper

1/2 cup pastini (tiny Italian soup pasta)

Freshly grated Romano cheese

❖ *B*rown sausage; drain. Add garlic and onion; saute until onion is transparent. Stir in carrots, zucchini, green pepper, wine, broth, tomatoes, basil, oregano and pepper. Bring to a boil. Add pastini and cook 20 minutes. Serve with Romano cheese and crusty French or Italian bread.

MINESTRONE

Servings: 8

1 **tablespoon minced garlic**

2 **tablespoons olive oil**

1 **cup finely chopped red onion**

1 **bay leaf**

3/4 **teaspoon dried sage, crushed**

3/4 **teaspoon dried rosemary, crushed**

2 1/2 **lbs. tomatoes, seeded and chopped**

1/4 **lb. fresh green beans, cut into 1/2-inch pieces**

1 **zucchini, cut into 1/2-inch cubes**

2 **carrots, cut into 1/4-inch slices**

1/2 **lb. new red potatoes, quartered**

1 **rib celery, cut into 1/4-inch slices**

1 **(19-oz.) can cannelli (white beans), drained**

5 **cups chicken broth**

1/2 **cup white wine**

1 **cup water**

1/3 **cup brown rice**

1/4 **cup minced fresh basil**

1/4 **cup minced fresh parsley**
    Salt and pepper, to taste

❖ *I*n 8-qt saucepan, saute garlic in olive oil for 1 minute. Add onion, bay leaf, sage and rosemary. Cook mixture until onion is softened. Add tomatoes, green beans, zucchini, carrots, potatoes and celery. Cook over moderate heat for 5 minutes. Stir in cannelli, chicken broth and wine. Bring mixture to a boil. Simmer covered 15 minutes. Add water and rice. Bring to a boil. Reduce heat and simmer covered for 15 to 20 minutes. Stir in basil and parsley. Add additional water to achieve desired consistency. Salt and pepper to taste.

    NOTE: This soup is even better when made a day ahead.

when served as
a main dish

FRENCH SEAFOOD SOUP

Servings: 4-6

3   tablespoons olive oil
1/2 cup chopped onion
2   cloves garlic, minced
1/2 cup chopped green pepper
1/2 cup chopped leeks
1/2 cup chopped carrots
1   dried red pepper, crushed or Tabasco sauce to taste
1   bay leaf
1/2 teaspoon dried thyme
1   cup white wine
1   cup chopped canned tomatoes
1/2 lb. potatoes, peeled and diced
1   cup water
1/2 pint fresh scallops
1   cup whipping cream
1/4 cup chopped fresh parsley
    Salt and pepper to taste
1 1/2 lb. cod, cut into large chunks
    Croutons

❖ *H*eat oil in medium saucepan. Add onion, garlic, pepper, leeks and carrots; saute until tender. Add red pepper, bay leaf, thyme, wine and tomatoes. Bring to a boil. Add potatoes; cook covered 10 minutes. Add water; cook uncovered 5 minutes or until potatoes are tender. Add scallops and simmer 2 to 3 minutes. Stir in cream. Bring to a boil, stirring constantly. Stir in parsley, salt and pepper. Add cod. Cook 5 minutes. Serve topped with croutons.

ERMA BOMBECK

CHICKEN and FLOUR TORTILLA DUMPLINGS

Servings: 6

1   (3-lb.) chicken, cut into pieces
    Water
    Salt
    Peppercorns
1   cup chopped celery
1   cup sliced carrots
1/2 cup chopped onion
2-3 teaspoons instant chicken bouillon
4-5 flour tortillas, cut into strips
    All-purpose flour

❖ *P*lace chicken in 3-quart saucepan or Dutch oven. Cover with water. Add salt, peppercorns, celery, carrots and onion. Add chicken bouillon. Bring to a boil. Reduce heat, cover and simmer 1 hour or until meat falls off bones. Skim fat off top while cooking, if necessary. Meanwhile, dust tortilla strips with flour. With tongs, remove chicken bones from saucepan. Bring broth to boil. Add floured tortilla strips and boil 5 minutes. Cover, lower heat and simmer 5 minutes.

Nationally syndicated columnist, author and humorist

JANET VOINOVICH

JAN'S POTATO SOUP

Servings: 6

5 medium potatoes, peeled
4 slices bacon, fried and crumbled, reserve fat
1 medium onion, minced
3 tablespoons all-purpose flour

❖ Cook potatoes in salted water until tender. Drain and cool; reserve cooking liquid. Dice potatoes. In large saucepan, saute onion in bacon fat until translucent. Stir in flour. Cook until mixture has thickened and is golden brown in color. Stir in bacon. Add potatoes and reserved cooking liquid. Heat through. Add more water if soup is too thick.

Former First Lady, City of Cleveland,
1991 First Lady of Ohio.

CHILLED STRAWBERRY HERB SOUP

Servings: 6

3 cups strawberries, washed, hulled and sliced
3 tablespoons honey
1 cup water
1¼ cups Gewürztraminer wine
¼ cup freshly squeezed orange juice
2 tablespoons fresh lemon juice
2 teaspoons grated orange peel
¼ teaspoon allspice
2 tablespoons fresh thyme leaves, crushed
¼ cup creme fraiche
Sugar

❖ Puree 2 ½ cups strawberries in food processor or blender; pour into medium bowl. Stir in honey, water, wine, orange juice, lemon juice, orange peel and allspice. Add thyme and creme fraiche. Add sugar to taste. Stir in remaining strawberries. Chill thoroughly. Garnish with sprigs of thyme.

CREME FRAICHE: To make creme fraiche, combine equal parts of sour cream and whipping cream. Allow to set at room temperature for several hours or until thickened.

CHICKEN and
TORTELLINI SOUP

Servings: 8-10

3	tablespoons olive oil
2	lbs. chicken breasts
1	medium onion, chopped
3	ribs celery, sliced
4	medium carrots, sliced
2	cloves garlic, minced
1	medium zucchini, sliced
1	teaspoon dried basil
1/2	teaspoon dried oregano
1/4	teaspoon dried thyme
1/4	teaspoon dried sage
3	medium white potatoes, cut into 1-inch cubes
1	(28-oz.) can crushed tomatoes
1	(8-oz.) can tomato sauce
1	(46-oz.) can chicken broth
1	cup dry white wine
1	(12-oz.) pkg. cheese tortellini (fresh or frozen)
	Salt and pepper to taste

❖ *I*n 5-qt. saucepan, saute chicken in olive oil. Remove chicken and pour off all but 2 tablespoons drippings. Add onion, celery and carrots. Cook until soft but not brown, stirring often. Add garlic, zucchini, basil, oregano, thyme, sage, potatoes, tomatoes, tomato sauce, broth, wine and chicken. Bring to a boil. Reduce heat; cover and simmer 1 hour. Remove chicken. Cool and remove meat from bone. Cut into pieces and return to saucepan. Prepare tortellini according to package directions; drain. Stir in tortellini and salt and pepper to taste. Serve with crusty bread and a white wine.

A quiet moment at Shaker Lakes

QUINOA SALAD with GREEN OLIVE PESTO

Servings: 4-6

Pesto

1	large clove garlic
1/4	teaspoon salt
1/2	teaspoon Dijon mustard
	Juice of 1/2 lemon
1/2	cup olive oil
2	tablespoons white wine vinegar
3/4	cup chopped green olives
3/4	cup finely chopped fresh parsley
	Salt and freshly ground black pepper, to taste
1-2	teaspoons fresh oregano, finely chopped

Salad

3	tablespoons olive oil
1	medium onion, chopped
1	clove garlic, chopped
2	tablespoons water
3	tablespoons dry white wine
	Pinch saffron
1	cup chopped fresh parsley
1/2	cup chopped green olives
3	cups cooked quinoa*
4-6	Italian plum tomatoes, sliced

❖ *P*ESTO: Mash garlic and salt in small bowl. Stir in mustard and lemon juice. Whisk in oil and vinegar. Add olives, parsley, salt, pepper and oregano. Refrigerate.

SALAD: Saute onion in oil for 1 minute. Add garlic; saute for 2 minutes. Stir in water, wine, saffron, parsley and olives. Heat to boiling. Reduce heat to low; cook 5 minutes. Cool slightly. Place olive mixture in food processor or blender. Process until smooth. Combine olive mixture with quinoa and sliced tomatoes; toss. Chill slightly. Serve on lettuce leaves with pesto.

* Quinoa: Pale yellow seed slightly larger than a mustard seed. This grain has a sweet flavor and a soft texture.

MIXED GREENS and PEAR SALAD with WALNUT VINAIGRETTE

Servings: 4

Dressing

- **1 medium shallot**
- **1/2 cup extra virgin olive oil**
- **2 tablespoons walnut oil**
- **2 tablespoons red wine vinegar**
- **1 tablespoon Dijon mustard**
- **1/2 teaspoon sugar**
- **1/4 teaspoon salt**
- **Freshly ground pepper**

Salad

- **1 tablespoon walnut oil**
- **1/2 cup walnut pieces**
- **1 large firm bartlett pear, unpeeled, halved lengthwise and cored**
- **10 cups torn mixed greens**

❖ DRESSING: In food processor or blender, mince shallot. Add olive oil, walnut oil, vinegar, mustard, sugar, salt and pepper; process until well blended.

SALAD: Heat walnut oil in small skillet over medium heat. Add walnuts. Cook about 4 minutes or until light brown and fragrant, stirring frequently. Transfer to bowl; cool. Cut each pear half into 1/4-inch slices. Place in small bowl; pour dressing on top. Place mixed greens in salad bowl. Using slotted spoon, remove pear slices. Add dressing to the greens and toss gently. Divide greens between 4 plates. Arrange 3 to 4 pear slices on each, overlapping slightly. Sprinkle with walnuts.

JOEL GREY

ARUGULA SALAD

Servings: 4-6

Dressing
- 2 tablespoons balsamic vinegar
- 4 tablespoons virgin olive oil
- 1 teaspoon fresh lemon juice

Salad
- 4 cups arugula, cleaned and stems removed
- 4 plum tomatoes, sliced in wedges
- Freshly cracked black pepper

❖ DRESSING: Combine all dressing ingredients.

SALAD: Combine arugula and tomatoes. Add dressing; toss. Garnish with freshly cracked black pepper.

Cleveland born Oscar winning actor and dancer

STRAWBERRY and SPINACH SALAD with PECANS

Servings: 4-6

Dressing
- 1/2 cup sugar
- 2 teaspoons dry mustard
- 2 teaspoons salt
- 2/3 cup vinegar
- 3-4 green onions, chopped
- 2 cups vegetable oil
- 3 tablespoons poppy seeds

Salad
- 1 lb. fresh spinach, cleaned and torn
- 2 cups thinly sliced celery
- 1 pint fresh strawberries, halved
- 1 1/2 cups caramelized pecan halves

❖ DRESSING: Combine sugar, mustard, salt, vinegar and onions in food processor or blender until onions are pureed. With machine running, add oil in a slow steady stream. Mix until thick and smooth. Stir in poppy seeds. Refrigerate.

SALAD: Combine all ingredients in bowl. Pour dressing over salad; toss gently.

CARAMELIZED PECANS: To caramelize pecans, melt enough butter to just coat a heavy skillet. Add 1 cup sugar and 1 1/2 cups pecan halves. Cook until browned. Transfer to wax paper. Cool.

PEA SALAD

Servings: 10

1   (20-oz.) pkg. frozen peas, thawed

1   lb. bacon, fried, drained and crumbled

1/4 cup chopped green onion

1/4 cup chopped celery

1   teaspoon salt

1   teaspoon sugar

1   teaspoon pepper

3/4 cup mayonnaise

7   oz. slivered almonds or cashews

❖ *C*ombine all ingredients. Refrigerate until chilled.

FRESH SPINACH and BASIL SALAD

Servings: 4-6

6   cups fresh spinach leaves, cleaned and torn

2   cups fresh basil leaves, cleaned
     Balsamic vinegar, to taste

1/4 cup olive oil

3   cloves garlic, minced

1/4 cup grated Parmesan cheese

1/4 cup pine nuts, toasted
     Ground black pepper

❖ *T*oss spinach and basil together in large bowl. Sprinkle with vinegar. Saute garlic in oil over medium heat. Pour over salad; toss. Sprinkle with cheese and pine nuts. Season with pepper.

The Cleveland Museum of Art

DENNIS NAHAT

TABOULI

Servings: 6

1   cup cracked wheat

1   cup cold water

8   green onions, minced

2   large bunches parsley, minced

1/2   bunch mint, minced

1   bunch radishes, minced

4   large tomatoes, finely chopped

    Juice of 4 lemons

1/2   cup olive oil

    Salt and pepper, to taste

❖ *S*oak wheat in water for 30 minutes at room temperature. Squeeze dry by pressing between palms. Combine all ingredients, blending well. Serve with grape, lettuce or cabbage leaves or pita bread.

Artistic Director of The Cleveland Ballet

ITALIAN SALAD

Servings: 8

1/2   head iceberg lettuce, torn

1   medium head Romaine lettuce, torn

1   cup canned artichoke hearts, drained and coarsely chopped

1   cup thinly sliced red onion

2/3   cup roasted red peppers or pimento, well drained and thinly sliced

2/3   cup olive oil

1/3   cup red wine vinegar

1   tablespoon freshly ground black pepper

1   cup freshly grated Parmesan cheese

1   cup sliced hearts of palm

❖ *P*lace lettuce in large bowl. Add artichoke hearts, onion and peppers; toss to combine. In small bowl, combine oil, vinegar and pepper. Pour over salad. Add cheese and hearts of palm; toss well.

JAMBALAYA SALAD

Servings: 8

2 eggs

1/3 cup sherry wine vinegar

3 tablespoons whole grained mustard

1/2 teaspoon salt

2 teaspoons freshly ground pepper

2 cups vegetable oil

1 medium onion, finely chopped

1/2 teaspoon crushed hot red pepper

1 teaspoon dried thyme

2 bay leaves

2 cups chicken stock

1 cup brown rice

3 ribs celery, cut crosswise on the diagonal in 1/2-inch pieces

1 small red bell pepper, cut into 1-inch pieces

1 small green pepper, cut into 1-inch pieces

4 green onions, thinly sliced

1 1/2 cups cooked chicken, diced

1 large head iceberg lettuce, coarsely shredded

2 ripe tomatoes, cut into 6 wedges

18 large cooked shrimp, peeled and deveined

❖ Combine eggs, vinegar, mustard, 1/4 teaspoon salt and black pepper in food processor or blender. Process for 1 minute. With machine running, pour in 1 3/4 cups oil. Process until blended. Cover and refrigerate. In medium saucepan, heat 3 tablespoons oil. Add the onion and cook over moderate heat about 5 minutes, or until tender but not brown. Add hot pepper, thyme and bay leaves. Cook, stirring, for 2 to 3 minutes or until fragrant. Stir in chicken stock, 1/4 teaspoon salt and rice. Increase heat to medium-high and bring to a boil. Reduce the heat to low, cover pan and cook until rice is tender and the liquid is absorbed. Remove from heat and let stand, covered for 5 minutes. Transfer rice to a large bowl. Remove bay leaves and let stand, stirring occasionally until cool. Add the celery, green pepper, red pepper, onions, chicken and remaining 1 tablespoon oil. Toss well to mix. To serve, line plates or bowl with shredded lettuce. Mound rice salad on lettuce. Garnish with tomato wedges and shrimp. Drizzle some of the dressing over salad and serve with additional freshly ground pepper. Pass the remaining dressing.

Breads & Pasta

Tiffany dome in Society Bank lobby

Surely *everyone enjoys the divine pleasure of luscious homemade bread. What could be more special than an afternoon tea resplendent with biscuits and cakes or a Sunday brunch enhanced by the presentation of enticing pasta. In this chapter we offer you a collection of breads and pastas that are delicate in their simplicity and old fashioned in their goodness.*

This section has been underwritten through the generosity of IDEAL MACARONI.

OATMEAL BREAD

Yield: 3 loaves or 6 mini loaves

1½ cups old-fashioned oats
1 cup boiling water
3 tablespoons butter or margarine
1 cup cold water
¾ cup molasses
2 teaspoons salt
1 pkg. active dry yeast
¾ cup warm water (105 degrees F. to 115 degrees F.)
8 cups unbleached flour

❖ Combine oats, boiling water and butter in large bowl. Stir to melt butter. Add cold water, molasses and salt. Cool to lukewarm. Sprinkle yeast in warm water; stir to dissolve. Let stand for 5 minutes. Add to cooled oat mixture. Stir in as much flour as possible. Turn dough onto floured surface; knead in remaining flour by hand. Continue kneading until dough is smooth and elastic. Place dough in lightly greased bowl; turn to grease top. Cover with warm damp cloth and let rise until double in size. Grease 3 (8 x 4-inch) loaf pans. Punch down dough; shape into 3 loaves. Place in prepared pans. Cover with warm damp cloth and let rise until dough reaches tops of pans. Heat oven to 375 degrees. Bake for 45 minutes or until bread loaves sound hollow when tapped. Remove from pans and cool on rack. Bread may be baked in 6 mini loaf pans for 30 minutes or until bread loaves sound hollow when tapped.

NO KNEAD FRENCH BREAD

Yield: 2 loaves

1 pkg. active dry yeast
1½ cups warm water (105 degrees F. to 115 degrees F.)
1 tablespoon sugar
1½ teaspoons salt
1 tablespoon butter, melted
4 cups all-purpose flour

❖ Sprinkle yeast in ½ cup warm water; stir to dissolve. In large mixing bowl, combine 1 cup water, sugar, salt and butter. Add dissolved yeast and mix well. Add flour, 1 cup at a time; mixing well. Cover with towel. Stir after 10 minutes. Work the dough with a wooden spoon at 10 minute intervals a total of 5 times. Dough becomes less sticky each time it is stirred. Divide dough in half. Shape into 2 balls. Allow to rest 10 minutes. Roll each ball into a 12 x 9-inch rectangle. Starting with long end, roll dough tightly jelly roll style. Pinch ends and tuck under. Place on baking sheet. Score top 5 to 6 times diagonally. Cover with towel and let rise 1½ to 2 hours or until double in size. Heat oven to 400 degrees. Bake for 20 to 35 minutes or until golden brown. For a softer crust, brush with melted butter after removing from oven.

EASY DINNER ROLLS

Yield: 24 rolls

1   pkg. active dry yeast
1   cup plus 1 tablespoon warm water (105 degrees F. to 115 degrees F.)
1   teaspoon sugar
1/2   cup sugar
2   eggs, beaten
6   tablespoons butter or margarine
1   teaspoon salt
3   to 3 1/2 cups all-purpose flour

❖ *S*prinkle yeast in 1 tablespoon warm water. Stir in 1 teaspoon sugar; set aside. In large bowl, combine eggs and sugar. Melt butter in 1 cup warm water; add to egg mixture. Stir in dissolved yeast. Stir in salt and flour; mix well. Place dough in lightly greased bowl; turn to grease top. Cover with warm damp cloth and let rise until double in size. Punch down dough; shape as desired. Lightly grease cookie sheet or muffin tins. Place in prepared pans. Brush rolls with melted butter. Cover with warm damp cloth and let rise until double in size. Heat oven to 350 degrees. Bake for 20 minutes or until golden brown.

This page has been underwritten through the generosity of SQUIRE, SANDERS & DEMPSEY.

ELEGANT DINNER BREAD

Yield: 1 loaf

1   cup milk
1/2   cup butter
1   pkg. active dry yeast
1/4   cup warm water (105 degrees F. to 115 degrees F.)
2   eggs, beaten
1/2   cup sugar
1/2   teaspoon salt
3   cups all-purpose flour
1/2   cup butter, melted

❖ *S*cald milk with 1/2 cup butter. Sprinkle yeast in warm water; stir to dissolve. Beat together eggs, sugar and salt. Add milk mixture. Stir in 1/2 cup flour and dissolved yeast; mix well. Let rise, uncovered, 1 hour. Add 2 1/2 cups flour; mix well. Cover with damp cloth and store in refrigerator overnight. Remove from refrigerator 3 hours before baking. Let stand for 2 hours at room temperature. Pour 1/2 cup melted butter into Bundt pan. Pour batter evenly into pan. Let rise for 1 hour. Heat oven to 350 degrees. Bake for 30 to 35 minutes or until golden brown.

FRESH STRAWBERRY MUFFINS

Yield: 24 muffins

3¹/₂ cups all-purpose flour
1¹/₂ cups sugar
  1 teaspoon cinnamon
  1 teaspoon salt
  1 teaspoon baking soda
1¹/₄ cups vegetable oil
  4 eggs, beaten
  1 cup chopped pecans (optional)
  1 lb. fresh strawberries, cleaned and chopped

❖ *P*reheat oven to 375 degrees. Grease 24 muffin cups or line with paper baking cups. In large bowl, combine flour, sugar, cinnamon, salt and baking soda. Mix oil and eggs together; pour over dry ingredients. Mix gently until just moistened. Batter will be very thick and dry. Mix in pecans and strawberries until dry ingredients are moistened. Fill muffin cups almost to top. Bake at 375 degrees for 20 to 25 minutes.

This page has been underwritten through the generosity of THE HUNTINGTON NATIONAL BANK.

CRANBERRY PECAN MUFFINS

Yield: 12-18 muffins

  2 cups all-purpose flour
¹/₂ cup sugar
  1 tablespoon baking powder
¹/₂ teaspoon baking soda
¹/₂ teaspoon salt
  1 cup milk
¹/₂ cup butter or margarine, melted
  2 eggs
  1 cup fresh cranberries, cleaned
¹/₂ cup chopped pecans

❖ *P*reheat oven to 400 degrees. Grease muffin cups or line with paper baking cups. Combine flour, sugar, baking powder, baking soda and salt. In small bowl, combine milk, butter and eggs. Blend into dry ingredients; mix until just moistened. Stir in cranberries and pecans. Spoon into prepared muffin pan. Bake at 400 degrees for 15 to 20 minutes.

PEANUT BUTTER MUFFINS

Yield: 12 muffins

$1/2$	cup yellow cornmeal
$1^{1/2}$	cups all-purpose flour
$1/3$	cup firmly packed brown sugar
$1/2$	teaspoon salt
1	tablespoon baking powder
2	eggs
$2/3$	cup creamy or chunky peanut butter
$1^{1/3}$	cups milk
$1/4$	cup unsalted butter, melted

❖ *P*reheat oven to 425 degrees. Grease muffin cups or line with paper baking cups. In large bowl, combine cornmeal, flour, brown sugar, salt and baking powder. In small bowl, beat eggs. Add peanut butter; mix well. Slowly add milk to peanut butter mixture, stirring until smooth. Stir in melted butter. Add to dry ingredients; mix well. Spoon into prepared muffin cups. Bake at 425 degrees for 20 minutes.

VARIATION: Top each muffin with $1/2$ teaspoon jelly before baking.

MYSTERY DINNER ROLLS

Yield: 12 rolls

2	cups self-rising flour
1	teaspoon fine herbs, if desired
1	cup whole milk
6	tablespoons mayonnaise

❖ *P*reheat oven to 425 degrees. Grease muffin cups. Place flour and herbs in bowl. Mix milk and mayonnaise; add to flour. Stir until just moistened. Fill prepared muffin cups $2/3$ full. Bake at 425 degrees for 15 to 20 minutes or until golden.

Garfield's Monument

SWEET POTATO NUT BREAD

Yield: 2 loaves

2¹/₂   cups sugar

¹/₂   cup molasses

²/₃   cup vegetable oil

4   eggs, lightly beaten

1   (16-oz.) can sweet potatoes, drained and mashed

²/₃   cup water

3¹/₃   cups all-purpose flour

2   teaspoons baking soda

1¹/₂   teaspoons salt

1   teaspoon cinnamon

1   teaspoon ground cloves

¹/₂   teaspoon baking powder

1   cup chopped nuts

❖ *P*reheat oven to 350 degrees. Grease bottom only of 2 (9 x 5-inch) loaf pans. Combine sugar, molasses, oil, eggs, sweet potatoes and water. Stir in flour, soda, salt, cinnamon, cloves, baking powder and nuts. Pour into prepared pans. Bake at 350 degrees for 1 hour and 10 minutes or until toothpick inserted in center comes out clean. Cool; remove from pans. Cool completely before slicing.

CRANBERRY PUMPKIN BREAD

Yield: 2 loaves

2   eggs, slightly beaten

2   cups sugar

¹/₂   cup oil

1   cup canned pumpkin

2¹/₂   cups all-purpose flour

1   tablespoon pumpkin pie spice

1   teaspoon baking soda

¹/₂   teaspoon salt

1   teaspoon cinnamon

1   teaspoon nutmeg

1   cup chopped cranberries

❖ *P*reheat oven to 350 degrees. Grease 2 (8 x 4-inch) loaf pans. Combine eggs, sugar, oil and pumpkin; mix well. In large bowl, combine flour, pumpkin pie spice, soda, salt, cinnamon and nutmeg. Make well in center. Pour pumpkin mixture into well. Stir until dry ingredients are just moistened. Stir in cranberries. Pour batter into prepared pans. Bake at 350 degrees for 1 hour or until toothpick inserted in center comes out clean.

PUMPKIN BREAD

Yield: 1 loaf

- 1/2 cup butter or margarine, softened
- 1 cup sugar
- 1 teaspoon vanilla
- 2 eggs
- 1 1/2 cups all-purpose flour
- 1/2 teaspoon salt
- 1 teaspoon baking soda
- 1 teaspoon cinnamon
- 1/2 teaspoon nutmeg
- 1/4 teaspoon ground ginger
- 1/4 teaspoon ground cloves
- 3/4 cup canned pumpkin
- 1/2-3/4 cup miniature chocolate chips
- 1/2 cup chopped nuts

❖ *P*reheat oven to 350 degrees. Grease 8 x 4-inch loaf pan. Cream butter with sugar; add vanilla. Beat in eggs. Combine flour, salt, soda, cinnamon, nutmeg, ginger and cloves. Alternately add flour mixture and pumpkin to egg mixture. Stir in chocolate chips and nuts. Pour into prepared pan. Bake at 350 degrees for 1 hour or until toothpick inserted in center comes out clean. Cool; remove from pans. Cool completely on wire rack.

ZUCCHINI BREAD

Yield: 2 loaves

- 3 eggs
- 2 cups sugar
- 1 cup vegetable oil
- 2 cups grated zucchini
- 3 teaspoons vanilla
- 3 cups all-purpose flour
- 1 teaspoon soda
- 1 teaspoon salt
- 1/2 teaspoon baking powder
- 1 teaspoon nutmeg
- 1 tablespoon cinnamon
- 1 cup chopped walnuts
- 1 cup chopped raisins

❖ *P*reheat oven to 325 degrees. Grease and flour 2 (9 x 5 x 3-inch) loaf pans. In medium mixing bowl, beat eggs until light and frothy. Gradually add sugar and oil, beating continually. Stir in vanilla and zucchini. Sift flour with soda, salt, baking powder, nutmeg and cinnamon. Fold into batter. Stir in nuts and raisins. Pour batter into pans. Bake at 325 degrees for 1 hour or until toothpick inserted in center comes out clean. Cool; remove from pans. Cool completely on wire rack.

LEMON POPPY SEED COFFEE CAKE

Servings: 12

1/3 cup poppy seeds
  1 cup milk
  2 cups all-purpose flour, sifted
2 1/2 teaspoons baking powder
1/2 teaspoon salt
  1 cup unsalted butter, softened
  1 cup sugar
  3 egg yolks
  2 tablespoons fresh lemon juice
  3 egg whites

❖ Combine poppy seeds and milk in small saucepan. Heat to boiling. Remove from heat and let stand for 1 hour. Preheat oven to 350 degrees. Butter and lightly flour a 10-inch tube pan. Sift flour, baking powder and salt in medium bowl. Cream butter and sugar until light and fluffy. Add egg yolks, one at a time, beating well after each addition. Add poppy seeds and milk. Fold in flour and lemon juice. Beat egg whites until stiff. Gently fold into batter. Spoon into prepared pan. Bake at 350 degrees for 50 minutes or until cake begins to pull away from sides of pan. Cool on rack for 10 minutes; invert onto cake plate. Cool completely before slicing.

LEMON BREAD

Yield: 1 loaf

  5 tablespoons butter or margarine, softened
  1 cup sugar
  1 teaspoon salt
  2 eggs
     Rind of 1 lemon, grated
1 1/2 cups sifted all-purpose flour
  1 tablespoon baking powder
1/2 cup milk
1/2 cup walnuts, chopped
     Juice of 1 lemon
1/2 cup sugar

❖ Preheat oven to 350 degrees. Grease 9 x 5-inch loaf pan. In medium mixing bowl, cream butter, 1 cup sugar and salt. Add eggs and lemon rind; beat well. Add flour, baking powder, milk and walnuts; beat well. Pour into prepared pan. Bake at 350 degrees for 1 hour. Cool on rack. In small bowl, combine lemon juice and 1/2 cup sugar. Pour over bread while still warm. When bread is cool, remove from pan, wrap in foil and refrigerate 24 hours.

LEMON BLUEBERRY TEA CAKE

Yield: 1 loaf

Topping

- 1/2 cup sugar
- 1/3 cup all-purpose flour
- 4 tablespoons unsalted butter, softened
- 2 teaspoons grated lemon rind
- 1 teaspoon cinnamon

Cake

- 3/4 cup sugar
- 1/2 cup milk
- 4 tablespoons unsalted butter, softened
- 1 egg
- 2 cups all-purpose flour
- 2 teaspoons baking powder
- 1/4 teaspoon salt
- 2 cups fresh blueberries
- 1 tablespoon grated lemon zest

❖ *T*OPPING: In a small bowl, combine all topping ingredients; set aside.

CAKE: Preheat oven to 375 degrees. Oil a 9 x 5-inch loaf pan. In medium bowl, beat sugar, milk, butter and egg until smooth. Combine flour, baking powder and salt. Stir into milk mixture. Fold in blueberries and lemon rind. Pour into prepared pan. Sprinkle with topping mixture. Bake at 375 degrees for 50 minutes or until topping is a deep golden brown and has formed a thick crust. Cool in pan for 5 minutes; transfer bread to wire rack until completely cool.

SOUR CREAM COFFEE CAKE

Servings: 8-12

Topping

- 1 cup chopped pecans or walnuts
- 1 cup firmly packed brown sugar
- 1 teaspoon cinnamon

Cake

- 8 pecan halves
- 1 cup butter, softened
- 2 cups sugar
- 2 eggs
- 2 cups sifted all-purpose flour
- 1 teaspoon baking powder
- 1 teaspoon baking soda
- 1/8 teaspoon salt
- 1 cup sour cream
- 1 teaspoon vanilla

❖ *T*OPPING: Combine nuts, brown sugar and cinnamon; set aside.

CAKE: Preheat oven to 350 degrees. Generously grease a 10-inch Bundt pan. Press a pecan half into each indentation in pan. In large bowl, cream butter and sugar until light and fluffy. Beat in eggs. Sift together flour, baking powder, baking soda and salt. Gradually stir dry ingredients into egg mixture; mix well. Fold in sour cream and vanilla. Sprinkle 2 tablespoons topping in bottom of prepared pan. Spoon 1/3 of batter over topping. Repeat layers. Bake at 350 degrees for 55 to 60 minutes or until toothpick inserted in center comes out clean. Cool on rack 10 minutes; invert onto serving plate.

BROCCOLI CORN BREAD

Servings: 6

3/4   cup cottage cheese

1   (10-oz.) pkg. frozen chopped broccoli, thawed and drained

1   teaspoon salt

1   large onion, chopped

1/2   cup butter or margarine

4   eggs, beaten

1   (8.5-oz.) box Jiffy cornbread mix

❖ *P*reheat oven to 350 degrees. Grease 9 x 13-inch pan. Combine cottage cheese, broccoli, salt, onion, butter and eggs. Stir in cornbread mix. Spread in prepared pan. Bake at 350 degrees for 40 to 45 minutes.

STUFFED ARTICHOKE BREAD

Servings: 8-12

1   loaf Italian or French bread

1/2   cup butter or margarine

6   cloves garlic, crushed

2   tablespoons sesame seeds

1 1/2   cups sour cream

2   cups Monterey Jack cheese, cubed

1/4   cup grated fresh Parmesan cheese

2   tablespoons parsley flakes

2   teaspoons lemon pepper

1   (14-oz.) can artichokes, drained and chopped

1   cup shredded sharp Cheddar cheese

❖ *P*reheat oven to 350 degrees. Line cookie sheet or jelly roll pan with foil. Cut bread in half lengthwise. Hollow out each half; tear bread into bite-sized pieces. Saute garlic in butter. Add bread pieces. Toss and stir until bread absorbs butter. In large bowl, combine bread mixture, sesame seeds, sour cream, Monterey Jack cheese, Parmesan cheese, parsley, lemon pepper and artichokes. Mound inside bread halves. Sprinkle with Cheddar cheese. Place bread halves on prepared baking sheet. Bake at 350 degrees for 30 minutes. To serve, slice in 2-inch pieces or cube and serve with toothpicks.

BLOSSOM
STUFFED BREAD

Servings: 8

2   **cloves garlic, minced**

4   **tablespoons butter**

1/2   **teaspoon nutmeg**

2   **(10-oz.) pkgs. frozen chopped spinach, thawed and squeezed dry**

1/2   **cup plus 2 tablespoons grated Parmesan cheese**

   Salt and pepper

2   **(4-oz.) jars roasted red peppers, drained**

8   **oz. Swiss cheese, sliced**

4   **oz. pepperoni, sliced**

1   **large round loaf Italian bread**

   Olive oil

❖ Preheat oven to 350 degrees. Saute garlic in butter. Add nutmeg, spinach and Parmesan cheese; toss until cheese melts. Season with salt and pepper. Cut off top 1/4 of bread; remove. Hollow out inside of bread, leaving a 1-inch crust. Place 1/3 of Swiss cheese in bottom. Layer as follows; 1/2 of spinach mixture, 1/3 Swiss cheese, 1/2 pepperoni, red peppers, 1/2 pepperoni, 1/3 Swiss cheese, 1/2 spinach and remaining cheese. Replace top. Rub exterior of loaf with olive oil. Wrap in foil. Bake at 350 degrees for 25 minutes. Cool. Serve at room temperature cut into wedges.

QUICK
MONKEY BREAD

Servings: 10

1/2   **cup chopped pecans**

1/2   **cup sugar**

1   **teaspoon cinnamon**

3   **(10-oz.) cans refrigerated buttermilk biscuits**

1   **cup firmly packed brown sugar**

1/2   **cup butter or margarine, melted**

❖ Preheat oven to 350 degrees. Grease a 10-inch Bundt pan. Sprinkle pecans in bottom of prepared pan. Combine sugar and cinnamon. Cut biscuits in half. Roll each piece in cinnamon sugar mixture; layer in pan. Combine brown sugar and butter; pour over dough. Bake at 350 degrees for 30 to 40 minutes. Cool 10 minutes in pan. Invert onto serving platter.

MRS. FUSCO'S PASTA with BROCCOLI, etc.

Servings: 6-8

1/2 bunch broccoli, cut into florets
1/2 head cauliflower, cut into florets
3 small zucchini, sliced
4 cloves garlic, chopped
1/4 cup olive oil
      Salt and pepper, to taste
1 pound Penne pasta
3 tablespoons fresh basil, chopped
      Freshly grated Parmesan cheese

❖ *F*ill large saucepan with water; bring to a boil. Add broccoli, cauliflower and zucchini. Cook until crisp-tender. Remove vegetables with slotted spoon; reserve water. Place olive oil in skillet or wok. Add garlic and saute for several minutes, being careful not to burn. Add vegetables, salt and pepper. Toss vegetables to coat with oil. Cook until vegetables are heated through. Bring vegetable water to a boil; add pasta. Cook until al dente; drain. Place pasta in large bowl. Add vegetables and basil. Toss to combine. Top with freshly grated Parmesan cheese.

Ohio born comedian and actor

PASTA with SAUSAGE and RED PEPPERS

Servings: 6

2 lbs. sweet Italian sausage
3 tablespoons olive oil
3/4 cup finely chopped onion
1 cup dry red wine
1 (6-oz.) can tomato paste
3 sweet red peppers, seeded and cut into 2-inch strips
1 cup water
1 tablespoon dried thyme
1 tablespoon dried oregano
1 1/2 teaspoons dried red pepper flakes
1 teaspoon dried basil, crushed
5-6 cloves garlic, minced
      Salt and pepper
3/4 cup chopped Italian parsley
1 lb. rigatoni

❖ *P*ierce sausage casings with fork. Place sausage in Dutch oven with 1/2-inch water. Cook over medium heat for 20 minutes. Turn and cook sausage additional 10 minutes. Remove sausage; drain fat from pan. Cook onions in oil over low heat for 15 minutes. Add peppers; cook 5 minutes. Add water, thyme, oregano, pepper flakes, basil and garlic. Simmer partially covered for 30 minutes. Cut sausage into 1/2-inch slices; add to Dutch oven. Add parsley and salt & pepper to taste. Simmer uncovered 20 minutes. Prepare rigatoni as directed on package. Top rigatoni with sausage mixture. Serve immediately.

Mr. & Mrs. Jahja Ling

SPICY SZECHUAN TOSSED NOODLES

Servings: 6

1   lb. dry Chinese noodles
4   tablespoons sesame paste
4   tablespoons soy sauce
1   tablespoon sugar
1   tablespoon sesame oil
1   tablespoon Worcestershire sauce
4   tablespoons hot pepper oil
1   tablespoon chopped green onion
1   tablespoon chopped ginger
1   tablespoon chopped garlic

❖ Cook noodles in boiling water until soft; drain. Combine all remaining ingredients; blending well. Pour over noodles and toss lightly.

Mr. Ling is Resident Conductor of The Cleveland Orchestra

International Horse Show

SPINACH FETTUCINI
with CHICKEN

Servings: 6

2 tablespoons butter

2-3 cloves garlic, pressed

1/4 cup virgin olive oil

2 whole chicken breasts, boned, skinned and cut into 1/2-inch strips

12 oz. shitake or porcini mushrooms

3/4 cup whipping cream

3/4 cup freshly grated Parmesan cheese

1/2 teaspoon freshly ground pepper

1 cup tomato, peeled and chopped

10 oz. fresh spinach fettucini (1 lb. dried)

1 teaspoon chopped parsley

❖ *I*n large skillet, saute chicken with butter, garlic and olive oil for about 8 minutes. Add mushrooms; saute 5 minutes. Reduce heat to medium-low. Add cream and Parmesan cheese, stirring constantly just until sauce thickens very slightly. Add tomatoes and pepper. Prepare fettucini as directed on package; drain. Place fettucini in large serving bowl. Add chicken mixture and toss well. Garnish with parsley.

BROCCOLI and
CHICKEN ALFREDO

Servings: 6

1 bunch broccoli, cut into florets

2 cloves garlic, crushed

3 tablespoons oil

4 whole chicken breasts, skinned, boned and cubed

8 oz. spinach fettuccine

1/2 cup butter

1 cup light cream

3/4 cup Parmesan cheese

1/2 cup shredded Mozzarella cheese

❖ *P*reheat oven to 350 degrees. Grease 9 x 13-inch pan. Steam broccoli for 5 minutes. Saute garlic in oil. Add chicken and cook until tender. Prepare fettuccine as directed on package; drain. In large saucepan, melt butter. Add cream, fettuccine, broccoli, chicken and Parmesan cheese. Heat through. Pour into prepared pan. Top with Mozzarella cheese. Bake at 350 degrees for 15 to 20 minutes or until heated through.

FOUR CHEESE PASTA
with PINE NUTS

Servings: 6

1   tablespoon butter

1/2 cup pine nuts

1/4 cup unsalted butter

1/4 cup grated Fontina cheese

1/4 cup grated Mozzarella cheese

1/4 cup grated Gruyere cheese

1/4 cup grated Parmesan cheese

1   cup whipping cream

1   lb. spinach fettucine

❖ *I*n small skillet, gently brown pine nuts in butter; set aside. Melt unsalted butter in heavy saucepan. Stir in Fontina, Mozzarella and Gruyere cheese. Cook over low heat until just melted. DO NOT OVERCOOK or cheese will become stringy. Add Parmesan cheese. Slowly add cream, whisking until smooth. Remove from heat. Cook pasta until al dente; drain. In large bowl, toss pasta with cheese sauce. Sprinkle with pine nuts and serve.

ANGEL HAIR PASTA
with TOMATO
and BASIL SAUCE

Servings: 6

2   lbs. fresh plum tomatoes, peeled, seeded and chopped

3/4 cup fresh basil leaves, coarsely chopped

1   (3¼-oz.) jar capers, rinsed and drained

3   tablespoons sherry vinegar (2 tablespoons vinegar + 1 tablespoon sherry)

1/2 teaspoon salt

1/2 teaspoon freshly ground pepper

1   (12-oz.) pkg. angel hair pasta

1/2 cup olive oil

❖ *C*ombine tomatoes with basil and refrigerate overnight. (Tomatoes and basil may be combined and marinated at room temperature several hours before dish is prepared.) Add capers, vinegar, salt and pepper. Marinate at room temperature for 2 hours. To serve, prepare pasta as directed on package. Drain and transfer to shallow bowl. Toss with 1/2 cup olive oil. Add tomato mixture and serve.

Mentor Headlands Beach on Lake Erie

The mere thought of seafood is enough to evoke *silent mists, soft breezes, and endless stretches of white sand. One of the beauties of seafood is discovered in the simplicity of its preparation. It is* natural, beautiful, simple and good for you. Our collection of recipes reflects "quick cuisine" enhanced by a taste for adventure .

JOSEPHINE R. ABADY

HOT and SOUR FISH SOUP

Servings: 8

4   cups chicken stock

4   tablespoons cornstarch

1/2   cup water

1/3   cup white vinegar

1/4   teaspoon cayenne pepper

1/4   teaspoon white pepper

4-6   tablespoons soy sauce

3   tablespoons sesame oil

2   eggs, beaten

1   lb. haddock, cubed

1   cup chopped green onions

❖ *In* large saucepan, bring chicken stock to a boil. Combine cornstarch with water to form a smooth paste. Whisk cornstarch into chicken stock. Add vinegar, pepper, soy sauce and sesame oil. Slowly add eggs, stirring briskly. Add fish; simmer 30 minutes. Taste and adjust seasonings. Soup should be slightly thick. Add more cornstarch dissolved in water to thicken. Just before serving, add green onions.

Former Artistic Director of The Cleveland Play House

FETTUCCINE al FRUTTI de MARE

Servings: 4-6

1   lb. medium shrimp, peeled and deveined

1/2   lb. scallops

1   cup fresh mushrooms, quartered

4   tablespoons butter

2/3   cup dry white wine

1   lb. fettuccine

4   tablespoons butter, softened

2 1/2   cups freshly grated Parmesan cheese

1   cup whipping cream

❖ *In* a heavy saucepan, saute shrimp, scallops and mushrooms in 4 tablespoons butter just until seafood is cooked. Add wine and cook until liquid is reduced to a sauce consistency; set aside.

Cook fettuccine in boiling, salted water until al dente. Drain and return to pan. Add softened butter to fettuccine; toss gently. Add cheese and cream. Toss together until cream sauce coats pasta. Transfer fettuccine to serving platter; top with seafood.

Wine Suggestion -
White: Italian; *Pinot Grigio*
White: California; *Acacia Vineyards;* Chardonnay

MIDWEST
BOUILLABAISE

Servings: 8 to 10

1   (1 to 1½ lb.) lobster or 2 lobster
     tails (4-6 oz.)

⅓   cup olive oil

¾   cup chopped onion

¾   cup chopped leeks

¾   cup chopped celery, with leaves

1-2   cloves garlic

1   lb. cod, flounder, haddock, red
     snapper, trout or walleye fillets,
     cut into 2-inch pieces

3   cups fish stock

1   cup water

1   (48-oz.) can tomatoes, cut up,
     reserve juice

1   tablespoon whole dried thyme

1   tablespoon whole dried marjoram

1   bay leaf, crumbled

2   teaspoons coarse salt
     Freshly ground pepper
     Pinch cayenne pepper

¾   lb. shrimp, peeled and deveined

½   cup dry white wine

❖ *I*n large pot, simmer live lobster until tender. Discard head. Set claws aside for another use. Cut lobster meat into large pieces. (If using lobster tail, cook until shells turn bright red. Remove from pot. Cut lobster meat into large pieces.)

Saute onion, leek, celery and garlic in olive oil until tender but not browned. Add fish, fish stock, water, tomatoes, thyme, marjoram, bay leaf, salt and pepper. Bring to a boil; reduce heat and simmer over low for 30 minutes. Add shrimp, wine and reserved tomato juice. Simmer 10 minutes. Add lobster; heat through. Serve with crusty French bread.

Wine Suggestions –
Red: French; *Gigondas Rhone*
White: French *Chateauneuf du Pape*

This page has been underwritten through the generosity of JOYCE LITZLER.

RIESLING TROUT

Serves: 4

4   (8-oz.) trout fillets
    Salt
    Freshly ground black pepper
    Flour
1/4 cup butter
3   shallots, minced
1   cup dry Riesling wine
1 1/4 cups creme fraiche
1 1/2 teaspoons fresh chervil, minced
1 1/2 teaspoons fresh chives, minced
1   teaspoon fresh tarragon, minced
1   teaspoon fresh parsley, minced
    Paprika

❖ *P*reheat oven to 400 degrees. Butter a 9 x 13-inch baking dish. Rinse trout in water and pat dry. Sprinkle with salt and pepper; cover with flour. In large skillet, melt butter over medium heat; add trout. Cook 2 minutes per side; remove skillet from heat. Transfer trout to prepared dish. Reduce heat to medium-low. Add shallots to skillet and cook until translucent; about 5 minutes. Add Riesling to skillet and bring to a boil, scrapping up brown bits from bottom of pan. Mix in creme fraiche, chervil, chives, tarragon and parsley; bring to a boil. Season with salt, pepper and paprika to taste. Pour mixture over trout.

Bake at 400 degrees for about 8 minutes or until fish is opaque, basting frequently. Transfer trout to heated platter. Heat sauce until reduced to 1 1/2 cups. Pour over trout to serve.

Wine Suggestions -
White: German; *Wehlenur Sonnenuhr;* Moselle Riesling
White: Alsace; Pinot Blanc or Riesling

GRILLED BLACK SEA BASS with BLACK BEAN MARINADE

Serves: 2-3

Marinade

- ¹/₂ **cup fermented black beans, minced**
- ¹/₂ **cup soy sauce**
- ¹/₄ **cup vegetable oil**
- 3 **tablespoons Chinese rice wine or dry sherry**
- 2 **tablespoons fresh ginger, peeled and minced**
- 1 **tablespoon sesame oil**
- ¹/₂ **teaspoon Chinese hot oil or 1 tsp. dried red pepper flakes**
- ¹/₂ **teaspoon sugar**

- 1 **(2-lb.) whole black sea bass**
- 2 **green onions, sliced julienne**
- 1 **lemon, thinly sliced**

❖ MARINADE: In large non-aluminum pan or bowl, combine marinade ingredients.

Slash both sides of fish four times, about ³/₄ inch deep, diagonally against body. Place fish in pan and spoon marinade over fish. Marinate for at least 1 hour, turning fish once.

Prepare grill. Cook fish approximately 7 minutes per side; basting frequently with marinade. Remove to a heated platter. Sprinkle fish with green onion and garnish with lemon slices.

NOTE: Any meaty fish such as walleye can be substituted for the bass.

Wine Suggestions -
White: California; *Kistler Vineyard;* Chardonnay
White: Australia; *Hunter Valley Reserve;* Chardonnay

LaDue Resevoir

Kenneth Francis Bates

ESCALLOPED OYSTERS NEW ENGLAND

Servings: 4- 6

1   pint large fresh oysters

1   tablespoon butter or margarine

1   tablespoon flour

3/4   cup milk

    Salt and freshly ground pepper to taste

6-8   unsalted soda crackers, coarsely crushed

1   tablespoon chopped fresh parsley

4-6   tablespoons butter

❖ *P*reheat oven to 350 degrees. Strain oysters, reserving liquid. Check carefully for bits of shell. Melt 1 tablespoon butter in saucepan. Stir in flour, milk and reserved oyster liquid. Salt and pepper to taste. Stir over medium heat until sauce is smooth and thickened. In 1-quart baking dish, layer crackers, oysters and cream sauce. Continue layering ingredients, ending with cracker crumbs. Dot with butter. Bake at 350 degrees for 25 to 30 minutes. Serve hot. Garnish with paprika and fresh parsley, if desired.

Wine Suggestions -
White: French; Chablis 1st Cru.
White: California; *Iron Horse*; Chardonnay

Internationally distinguished Enamelist

HICKORY SMOKED TROUT

Servings: 4- 6

1-2   handfuls hickory chips

1   whole fresh trout, room temperature

1   tablespoon butter, melted

1/8   teaspoon fresh dill

2   teaspoons white wine Worcestershire sauce

1   lemon, thinly sliced

    Salt to taste

    Non-stick cooking spray

    Olive oil

❖ *S*oak hickory chips in enough water to cover. Prepare charcoal grill. Grill is ready when coals are red hot.

Brush melted butter on inside fish cavity. Season with dill, white wine Worcestershire and salt. Place lemon slices inside fish cavity. Spray fish rack with non-stick spray. Lightly coat fish with olive oil. Place fish on rack. Remove hickory chips from water and place on top of hot coals. Place the fish rack on the grill. Cover grill and cook fish about 4 to 5 minutes per side.

VARIATION: Salmon may be substituted for trout. Omit olive oil and use tarragon in place of dill. Serve with corn on the cob.

Wine Suggestions -
White: German; *Rhinegau;* Riesling Spatlese.
White: Washington; Johannisberg Riesling

SCALLOPS
with VERMICELLI

Servings: 4

1½   lbs. bay or sea scallops, rinsed
     and drained

3   tablespoons fresh lemon juice

2   tablespoons fresh parsley

1   tablespoon oil

2   tablespoons unsalted butter

1   onion, chopped

1   clove garlic, minced

¼   teaspoon dried oregano, crushed

¼   teaspoon dried thyme

2   tablespoons finely chopped
     fresh basil leaves

2   (14-oz.) cans plum tomatoes,
     drained and chopped, reserve
     juice

¾   lb. vermicelli

2   tablespoons whipping cream

     Nutmeg

     Salt and pepper

❖ Combine scallops, lemon juice
and parsley; marinade at room temperature for
45 minutes.

In medium saucepan, saute onion and
garlic in oil and 1 tablespoon butter over
moderate-low heat; until onion is soft. Add
oregano, thyme, basil and chopped tomatoes.
Simmer covered for 30 minutes, stirring
occasionally.

Cook vermicelli as directed on
package; drain well. Saute scallops in 1
tablespoon butter over moderately-high heat
for 2 minutes. Add cream, nutmeg, tomato
mixture, and enough of the reserved tomato
juice to thin to desired consistency. Add salt
and pepper to taste. Bring to a boil, stirring
constantly; remove from heat Toss with
vermicelli and serve.

Wine Suggestions -
White: California; *Duckhorn;* Sauvignon Blanc
White: Italian; *Orvieto Secco*

SCALLOPS du CHEF

Servings: 8

1/4	cup unsalted butter
3/4	lb. mushrooms, sliced 1/4-inch thick
6	tablespoons dry white wine
1	(8-oz.) pkg. cream cheese, softened
2	teaspoons flour
2	teaspoons butter, softened
	Salt
	Freshly ground pepper
2	eggs, lightly beaten
2	lbs. bay scallops, chilled and patted dry
3/4	cup butter, melted
16	sheets phyllo dough

❖ *S*aute mushrooms in 1/4 cup butter until tender, about 4 to 5 minutes. Remove with slotted spoon. Add wine to skillet, increase heat and cook until liquid is reduced by half. Reduce heat to low and add cream cheese, stirring until melted. Bring mixture to a gentle simmer. In small bowl, combine flour and 2 teaspoons butter. Slowly whisk in flour mixture blending until smooth. Season with salt and pepper to taste. Cool. Beat in eggs. Fold in mushrooms and scallops. Preheat oven to 400 degrees. Butter baking sheet or line with parchment paper. Lay sheet of phyllo on work surface. Brush with melted butter, top with second phyllo sheet. Spoon 1/8 of scallop mixture in strip along short end of phyllo, leaving a 2-3 inch margin on each side. Roll up short end tightly until 2/3 rolled. Fold in sides of phyllo and brush remaining 1/3 dough with butter. Continue rolling. Place seam side down on baking sheet and brush lightly with butter. Repeat with remaining ingredients. Bake at 400 degrees for 15 to 20 minutes or until golden brown. Serve with herbed rice.

Wine Suggestions -
White: French; *CH.Carbonnieux;* Bordeaux
White: California; *Iron Horse;* Chardonnay

BUFFET
SHRIMP CURRY

Servings: 4-6

2 cups mayonnaise

1¼ cups milk

¼ cup butter or margarine

½ cup chopped onion

¼ cup chopped green pepper

2 cloves garlic

1 tablespoon curry powder

2 teaspoons lemon juice

¾ teaspoon salt

½ teaspoon ground ginger

3 cups cooked shrimp, halved lengthwise

❖ Combine mayonnaise and milk. Melt butter in large skillet over medium heat. Add onion, green pepper, garlic and curry powder; saute until vegetables are tender, stirring frequently. Remove skillet from heat and stir in mayonnaise mixture, lemon juice, salt, ginger and shrimp. Return skillet to low heat. Heat through for 10-15 minutes, stirring occasionally. Serve with rice and assorted accompaniments such as sauteed onions, toasted coconut, chutney, mandarin orange segments, pineapple tidbits, raisins, peanuts or tomato.

Wine Suggestions -
White: Alsation; Pinot Blanc
White: California; Dry Riesling or Gewürztraminer

TEX-MEX SHRIMP
FETTUCCINE

Servings: 6

1½ cups butter or margarine

2 medium onions, chopped

2 green peppers, chopped

3 ribs celery, chopped

6 cloves garlic, minced

2 tablespoons chopped fresh parsley

3 lbs. raw shrimp, peeled and deveined

¼ cup flour

2 cups half-and-half

1½ lbs. Mexican Velveeta cheese, cubed

1 lb. fettuccine

Parmesan cheese

❖ Preheat oven to 350 degrees. Saute onions, peppers, celery and garlic in butter until vegetables are tender. Add parsley and shrimp; cook for 10 minutes. Add flour, half-and-half and Mexican cheese. Simmer over low heat 30 minutes. Prepare fettuccine according to package directions; rinse and drain. Add fettuccine to cheese mixture. Spread mixture in 13 x 9-inch pan. Sprinkle top with parmesan cheese. Bake at 350 degrees covered for 30 minutes or until bubbly. Remove cover and bake additional 10 minutes.

Wine Suggestions-
White: *Husch Vineyard;* Gewürztraminer
White: German; *Rhinegau;* Riesling Spatlese

WULF UTIAN

SEASONED BAKED FISH

Servings: 6

6 thick cod or halibut steaks,
    rinsed and patted dry
    Juice of 1 lemon
    Salt and freshly ground pepper
2 large onions, sliced
1/2 cup olive oil
2 cloves garlic, crushed
4 large tomatoes, peeled,
    seeded and chopped
1/2 cup dry white wine
3 tablespoons chopped fresh basil
1 cup olives (optional)

❖ Preheat oven to 300 degrees.
Place fish in oven proof dish. Sprinkle with
lemon juice. Generously season with salt
and pepper. Saute onions in 1/4 cup olive oil
until tender but not browned. Add garlic,
tomatoes and wine. Simmer gently for about
30 minutes or until reduced and mixture has
thickened slightly. Season with salt and
pepper to taste. Pour mixture over fish.
Sprinkle with basil and olives. Drizzle 1/4
cup olive oil over top. Bake at 300 degrees
for 40 minutes or until fish flakes easily
when tested with a fork. May be served hot
or cold.

*Fertility expert and founder of
the world's first Menopause Clinic*

SHRIMP CREOLE

Serves: 6

2 tablespoons butter
1/2 cup chopped celery
1/2 cup chopped red pepper
1/2 cup chopped mushrooms
1/2 cup chopped onion
1/2 cup chopped carrots
1/2 cup chopped green beans
1 clove garlic, crushed
    Salt and pepper, to taste
1 tablespoon Kitchen Bouquet
1 teaspoon paprika
1 teaspoon crushed chili pepper
1/4 teaspoon dry mustard
2 teaspoons tomato paste
1/4 teaspoon curry powder
3 teaspoons flour
1/2 cup shrimp stock
1/2 cup dry white wine
2 lbs. shrimp, cooked
1 cup sour cream

❖ Melt butter in large saucepan.
Add celery, pepper, mushrooms, onion,
carrots, green beans and garlic. Season with
salt and pepper; saute until tender. Remove
from heat. Stir in Kitchen Bouquet, paprika,
chili pepper, dry mustard, tomato paste,
curry powder, flour, shrimp stock and white
wine. Cook over moderate heat until mixture thickens. Add shrimp; heat through.
Stir in sour cream. Do not boil, or sauce will
curdle. Serve with freshly cooked rice.

Wine Suggestions -
White: French; *Vouvray*
White: California; *Husch Vineyard*; Dry Chenin Blanc

SHRIMP and ARTICHOKE SUPREME

Serves: 6

1   (14-oz.) can artichoke hearts, drained and quartered

1½ lbs. fresh shrimp, boiled, shelled and deveined

3   tablespoons butter or margarine

1   clove garlic, crushed

1   onion, chopped or 3 green onions, chopped

4   oz. fresh mushrooms, sliced

1   (10-oz.) can cream of mushroom soup

½   cup mayonnaise

1   tablespoon Worcestershire sauce

2   tablespoons dry sherry

½   cup grated Parmesan cheese
    Salt and pepper, to taste

1   (10-oz.) pkg. frozen chopped spinach, thawed and drained
    Paprika
    Parmesan cheese

❖ *P*reheat oven to 375 degrees. Butter a 2-quart casserole. Place artichokes in prepared pan; add shrimp. In large fry pan, saute garlic, onion, and mushrooms in butter. Add soup, mayonnaise, Worcestershire sauce, sherry, cheese, salt and pepper. Add spinach; blend well. Pour mixture over shrimp. Sprinkle with additional Parmesan cheese and paprika. Bake at 375 degrees for 20 minutes. Garnish with parsley or bread crumbs. Serve over wild rice or puff pastry shells.

Wine Suggestions -
White: Italian; *Gavi di Gavi*
White: California; *Duckhorn Vineyard*; Sauvignon Blanc

SUSAN ORLEAN

QUICK MARSEILLES FISH STEW

Servings: 2

1   large onion, thinly sliced

1   teaspoon minced garlic

1   tablespoon olive oil

3/4   cup dry white wine

1   (14-oz.) can crushed tomatoes

3   tablespoons tomato paste

     Grated peel of 1/2 orange

1   teaspoon fennel seed

1   teaspoon dried thyme

1   small bay leaf

3/4   lb. fish fillet such as grouper, snapper or swordfish, cut into chunks

3/4   **pound tiny potatoes, skin on**

❖ *S*aute onion and garlic in oil until soft and golden. Add wine, tomatoes, tomato paste, orange peel, fennel, thyme and bay leaf. Cover and cook over medium heat for 10 minutes. Add fish and cook for 3 minutes, or until fish is done. Boil potatoes until tender, about 20 minutes. Drain; quarter potatoes. To serve, top potatoes with fish stew. Serve with a salad of peppery greens such as arugula or watercress.

Wine Suggestions -
Red: French; *Gigondas Rhone*
White: French; *Chateauneuf du Pape*

Noted author and journalist, frequent contributor to NY Times Magazine

SHRIMP ORLEANS

Servings: 4

1   tablespoon butter or margarine

1   medium onion, chopped

1/2   green pepper, chopped

1 1/2   lbs. (3 cups) cooked shrimp

1/2   cup sliced fresh mushrooms

1   (10-oz.) can cream of mushroom soup

1   cup sour cream

1   clove garlic, minced

1/2   cup ketchup

1/2   teaspoon celery salt

❖ *M*elt butter in large skillet over medium heat. Saute onion and green pepper until tender. Add shrimp, mushrooms, soup, sour cream, garlic, ketchup and celery salt. Simmer over medium heat for 15 minutes; do not boil. Serve over rice.

Wine Suggestions -
White: French; *Crozes Hermitage;* Rhone
White: California; *CH. St. Jean;* Chardonnay

SOLE
with HERBS and WINE

Servings: 4-6

Lemon-Herb Butter

3	tablespoons butter, softened
1/4	teaspoon grated lemon rind
1/4	teaspoon garlic powder
1/4	teaspoon dill
1/4	teaspoon oregano

Sole

2/3	cup all-purpose flour
3/4	teaspoon paprika
	Salt
2	tablespoons vegetable oil
1 1/2	lbs. sole fillets
3/4	cup dry white wine
1	teaspoon lemon juice
2	small carrots, cut into julienne strips
1/2	cup whipping cream
3	tablespoons Lemon-Herb butter
2	green onions, cut on the diagonal

❖ LEMON-HERB BUTTER: Combine butter and seasonings; chill.

SOLE: In shallow pan, combine flour, paprika and salt. Heat oil in large saute pan. Lightly dredge sole fillets in flour mixture and gently place them in pan; saute 2-3 minutes on each side. Remove to serving platter. Repeat until all fillets are cooked. Place saute pan over high heat; add wine, lemon juice and carrots; cook until liquid is reduced by half. Add cream and reduce liquid by half. Swirl in lemon-herb butter, reduce until sauce has thickened. Remove from heat, add green onions and pour over fish. Serve with rice, green salad and crusty bread.

Wine Suggestions -
White: French; Muscadet
White: California; *Beaulieu Vineyards*; Sauvignon Blanc

Sailing on Lake Erie

PAELLA a la
COSTA del SOL

Servings: 4

1   cup olive oil

10   cloves garlic, crushed

16   raw shrimp, peeled with tail remaining

2   swordfish steaks, cut into 2-inch cubes

3/4   cup peas, fresh or frozen

4   artichoke hearts, quartered

1   red pepper, sliced

    Salt & pepper

1/3   cup tomato paste

2   cups rice

4 1/2   cups chicken broth

1   teaspoon saffron threads

1   teaspoon Colorante* (if available)

16   mussels, steamed

❖ *I*n large skillet or wok, heat 1/4 cup olive oil. Add shrimp, 3 cloves garlic, salt and pepper to taste. Stir fry for 2 minutes. Shrimp should be slightly undercooked. Remove shrimp from pan; add 2 tablespoons olive oil. Add swordfish, 3 cloves garlic and salt and pepper; stir fry approximately 3 minutes. Fish should be slightly undercooked. Remove fish. If needed, add 2 tablespoons olive oil to pan. Add peas, artichoke hearts, red pepper, salt and pepper and cook approximately 4 minutes; remove and place in large bowl.

Heat 1/2 cup olive oil in palleria or large sauce pan over high heat. Add tomato paste to pan, stirring constantly; cook until bubbly. It is best to overcook the tomato paste slightly. Add rice and cook for 2-3 minutes, stirring constantly. Add chicken broth, saffron and Colorante (if available). Boil for 4 minutes. Add peas, artichokes, shrimp and fish; decorate the top with red peppers. Reduce heat to low and cover with lid or foil. Cook for 40-50 minutes or until rice is tender. If paella looks dry while cooking add additional broth or water. Top with mussels and serve with fresh lemon wedges.

VARIATION: Add cooked chicken or Italian sausage.

Colorante is a dry, yellow powder. Colorante is not for flavor, but rather gives yellow color to the dish. May substitute tumeric in place of colorante.

Wine Suggestions -
White: Spanish; *Rioja Marques de Caceres*
White: California; *Kenwood Vineyards;* Sauvignon Blanc
Red: French; *Côte du Rhone*
Sherry: Spanish; *Dry Oloroso (chilled)*

GRILLED SWORDFISH with LEMON CAPER BUTTER SAUCE

Servings: 6

6   (8-oz.) swordfish steaks,
    1-inch thick
    Olive oil

Sauce

2 1/2   cups dry white wine
    3   tablespoons shallots, minced
    1   cup unsalted butter, softened
    3   tablespoons small capers, drained
  2-3   tablespoons fresh lemon juice
        Freshly cracked pepper

❖ *P*repare grill. Brush swordfish lightly with olive oil. Place steaks on grill approximately 5-6 inches above coals. Grill 5-7 minutes on each side; remove to warm platter.

SAUCE: In small saucepan, combine wine and shallots. Heat until mixture is reduced to 1/2 cup. Lower heat and whisk in butter, two tablespoons at a time. Do not boil sauce. Stir in capers, lemon juice, and pepper. To serve, spoon sauce over fish or pass on the side. Sauce may be prepared ahead and reheated over low heat.

Wine Suggestions -
White: French; *Puligny Montrachet*
White: California; *Far Niente;* Chardonnay

GRILLED SWORDFISH with PIQUANT PARSLEY SAUCE

Servings: 4

3/4   cup Italian parsley, trimmed
      of stems
  2   cloves garlic
  1   tablespoon capers, rinsed
      and drained
1/4   cup chopped onion
  1   oz. anchovies, mashed or
      1 oz. anchovy paste
1/2   teaspoon freshly cracked pepper
  1   tablespoon balsamic vinegar
  1   tablespoon red wine vinegar
1/3   cup olive oil
  4   swordfish steaks, 1-inch thick

❖ *P*repare grill. In work bowl of food processor, finely chop parsley. Add garlic, capers, onion, anchovies and pepper; pulse until finely chopped (do not puree). In small bowl, combine the vinegars; slowly whisk in the oil to create an emulsion. With a whisk, combine the parsley mixture with the vinaigrette.

Grill steaks 7 to 10 minutes per side or until fish flakes easily with fork. To serve, spoon sauce over fish.

Wine Suggestions -
White: California; *Simi Reserve;* Chardonnay
White: French; *Sancerre*

A view of downtown Cleveland from Edgewater Park

We invite you to intrigue your guests with these savory and imaginative recipes created for the discriminating connoisseur. Our collection of recipes is intended to infuse a mark of individuality, challenge the traditional and entice your spirit of adventure.

This section has been underwritten through the generosity of APCOA, INC.

SUNDAY NIGHT
STRATA

Servings: 4-6

Marinade

- ⅓ **cup olive oil**
- 3 **tablespoons Worcestershire sauce**
- ¼ **teaspoon dried tarragon**
- ¼ **teaspoon dried marjoram**
- ¼ **teaspoon dry mustard**
  Salt and pepper

- 1 **lb. beef round, cut into 8 thin slices**
- 4 **tablespoons unsalted butter**
- 1 **tablespoon olive oil**
- 8 **very thin slices pepper-coated ham**
- 8 **very thin slices Gruyere cheese**
- 1 **cup sliced fresh mushrooms**
- 4 **tablespoons unsalted butter, melted**
- 1½ **tablespoon all-purpose flour**
- ⅓ **cup Madeira wine**
- ¼ **cup water**

❖ Combine marinade ingredients in shallow dish. Place beef slices in marinade. Cover and refrigerate 8 hours. Preheat oven to 400 degrees. Remove beef from marinade; reserve marinade. Place on paper towels and pat dry. Melt 2 tablespoons butter in large skillet with olive oil over high heat. Cook beef 1 minute on each side or until lightly browned. Drain on paper towels. Arrange 4 beef slices in bottom of oven proof dish. Cover with 4 slices of ham and cheese. Sprinkle mushrooms over cheese. Drizzle melted butter over mushrooms. Cover mushrooms with remaining ham and cheese. Top with remaining beef. Melt 2 tablespoons butter in small saucepan over medium heat. Add flour and cook for 1 minute, stirring constantly. Stir in reserved marinade, Madeira and water. Cook until thickened. Pour the sauce over beef layers and bake at 400 degrees for 10 minutes. Serve hot with crusty bread, dark green salad and baked lima beans or broccoli.

Wine Suggestions -
Red: French; *Cote Du Rhone*
Red: Italian; *Chianti Classico*

This page has been underwritten through the generosity of GEORGIA STONEHILL.

STUFFED SIRLOIN STEAK

Servings: 8

2   (1½ lb.) sirloin steaks, 1½-inches thick
1   onion, chopped
2   cloves garlic, minced
1   tablespoon butter
½   cup Burgundy wine
¼   cup Tamari soy sauce
1   cup fresh mushrooms, sliced
2   tablespoons butter

❖ Cut deep pockets on each side of sirloin. Saute onion and garlic in 1 tablespoon butter until tender. Stuff pockets with onion mixture. Skewer sides shut. Combine wine and soy sauce in pan large enough to lay both steaks flat in a single layer. Marinate the steaks 4 hours or overnight, turning occasionally. Heat barbecue grill. Grill over medium-hot coals 25 to 30 minutes for rare; baste frequently with marinade. Saute mushrooms in 2 tablespoons butter. Serve over meat.

Wine Suggestions -
Red: French; *Grands Echeleaux*
Red: California; *CH. Montelena*; Cabernet Sauvignon

DEVILED STEAK

Servings: 6-8

2   tablespoons Dijon mustard
2   teaspoons lemon juice
1   (2-3 lb.) sirloin steak, 2 to 3-inches thick
    Seasoned salt
¼   cup ketchup
¼   cup water
¼   cup olive oil
2   tablespoons red wine vinegar
2   tablespoons soy sauce
3   tablespoons plum or cherry jam
3   tablespoons firmly packed brown sugar
    Dash pepper
    Few drops Tabasco sauce

❖ Combine mustard and lemon juice. Spread mixture over both sides of steak. Sprinkle steak with seasoned salt. Combine remaining ingredients in medium saucepan. Heat to boiling; cool slightly. Pour sauce over steak. Allow to marinate in refrigerator 2 hours or overnight, turning occasionally. Remove meat from marinade. Heat barbecue grill. Grill 5 to 10 minutes per side, basting frequently.

Wine Suggestions -
Red: French; *Beaujolais Villages*
Red: California; *Beringer*; Gamay

INDIVIDUAL
BEEF WELLINGTONS

Servings: 8

8   (4-oz.) beef tenderloin fillets
1   clove garlic, minced
    Salt and pepper
1   teaspoon butter
2   teaspoons sherry

Filling
1/4 cup butter
1   lb. fresh mushrooms, chopped
1/2 cup dry sherry
1/2 cup chopped onions

Crust
1   pkg. puff pastry sheets, thawed
1   egg, beaten

Sauce
2   cups beef broth
3   teaspoons chopped onion
1   teaspoon chopped celery
1/8 teaspoon thyme
3   teaspoons chopped carrots
2   sprigs parsley
1/2 cup dry sherry
1   bay leaf
2   tablespoons butter
3   tablespoons dry sherry

❖ *H*eat oven to 425 degrees. Grease 15 x 10-inch jelly roll pan. Rub fillets with garlic, salt and pepper to taste. In large skillet, sear fillets in 1 teaspoon butter and 2 teaspoons sherry. Reserve pan drippings for filling. Drain fillets on paper towels. Refrigerate.

FILLING: Add 1/4 cup butter, chopped mushrooms, 1/2 cup sherry and 1/2 cup onions to pan drippings. Cook and stir until onion is tender and all liquid is absorbed. Spread equal portions of filling over top of each chilled steak. Refrigerate while preparing crust.

CRUST: Cut puff pastry into 8 squares. Place fillets, mushroom side down on pastry, enclosing it completely; seal edges with beaten egg. Place seam side down in prepared pan. Brush entire pastry with beaten egg. Bake at 425 degrees for 15 to 25 minutes or until crust is golden.

SAUCE: In large saucepan, combine broth, onions, celery, thyme, carrots, parsley, sherry and bay leaf. Simmer 1/2 hour. Strain, discarding vegetables. Stir in 2 tablespoons butter and 3 tablespoons sherry. Simmer 5 minutes.

Wine Suggestions -
Red: French; *CH. La Tour* or *CH. Troplong Mondat*
Red: California; *Opus I*; Cabernet Sauvignon
Red: French; *Clos de Vougeot*

SOUTHWESTERN FLANK STEAK

Servings: 6-8

1 (1 1/2 to 1 3/4 lb.) flank steak, butterflied

Marinade

3/4 cup lemon juice

3/4 cup vegetable oil

1/4 cup Worcestershire sauce

1 clove garlic, minced

Ground pepper

1 teaspoon liquid smoke

Filling

1 (8-oz.) pkg. frozen chopped spinach, thawed and well drained

8 oz. roasted red peppers, cut into strips

1 cup chopped onions

2 (4-oz.) cans chopped green chilies, drained

1 clove garlic, minced

1 teaspoon ground cumin

1 teaspoon chili powder

1/4 cup grated Monterey Jack cheese

❖ MARINADE: Combine all marinade ingredients. Place steak in plastic bag; pour marinade over steak. Refrigerate 8 hours or overnight.

Preheat oven to 350 degrees. Remove meat from marinade; pat dry. Place on counter with grain running horizontally.

Spread spinach over meat. Top with red peppers and onions. Combine chilies, garlic, cumin and chili powder. Sprinkle over meat. Top with grated cheese. Starting at nearest end, roll steak tightly. Tie in several places. Bake at 350 degrees for 45 minutes. Allow to rest 5 to 10 minutes before slicing.

Wine Suggestions -
Red: California; *Karly Vineyards*; Zinfandel
Red: French; *Gigondas*

Tower City

NO FAIL TENDERLOIN

Yield: 6-8 servings

1   whole beef tenderloin

Marinade

1   teaspoon salt
1   teaspoon pepper
2   teaspoons chopped chives
1/4 cup vegetable oil
3   tablespoons Dijon mustard
1   teaspoon sugar
1/4 cup soy sauce
3   tablespoons Worcestershire sauce
1/2 cup red wine

❖ *E*arly in the day, set roast out at room temperature. Combine all marinade ingredients; pour over beef. Refrigerate, covered for several hours, turning occasionally. Seven hours before you wish to serve, prepare barbecue grill. Remove roast from marinade. Cook roast on grill 6-7 minutes per side. Remove from grill; replace in pan with marinade. Cover tightly with foil. Allow to sit at room temperature about 6 hours. About 30 minutes before serving, preheat oven to 350 degrees. Bake at 350 degrees for 15 minutes (rare to medium rare), longer for medium to well done.

Wine Suggestions -
Red: French; *Wuits St. George*
Red: French; *CH. Gruaud Larose*
Red: California; *Jordon Vineyards;* Cabernet Sauvignon

GREEN PEPPERCORN SAUCE

Yield: 3 cups

9   beef bouillon cubes
2   cups hot water
1/2 cup butter
3   shallots, finely chopped
1/2 cup all-purpose flour
1/2 cup Madeira wine
1/4 teaspoon ground black pepper
1 1/2 teaspoons Kitchen Bouquet
2-4 tablespoons green peppercorns, drained
2/3 cup brandy
2/3 cup whipping cream

❖ *D*issolve beef bouillon cubes in hot water. In medium saucepan, saute shallots in butter until soft. Add flour and cook several minutes, stirring constantly. Slowly whisk in wine and beef stock. Add black pepper, Kitchen Bouquet and peppercorns. Simmer 15 minutes. Just before serving, heat brandy in heavy skillet over high heat. Using a long match, ignite brandy. After the flame has burned out, stir in beef stock mixture and whipping cream. Heat through. Serve with beef tenderloin.

VARIATION: Also excellent served with filet mignon. Cook steaks until just rare; finish cooking meat in completed sauce.

SKILLET MEATLOAF with WILD MUSHROOMS

Servings: 4

1   oz. dried imported mushrooms
1   cup warm water
1   lb. lean ground sirloin
1   tablespoon chopped onion
    Salt and pepper, to taste
2   tablespoons chopped Proscuitto, Pancetta or Mortadella
1/2 cup grated Parmesan cheese
2   cloves garlic, finely minced
1   egg yolk
1/2 cup fine dry bread crumbs
1   tablespoon butter
2   tablespoons olive oil
1/3 cup dry white wine
2   tablespoons tomato paste

❖ *S*oak mushrooms in warm water for 20 minutes. Combine ground sirloin, onion, salt, pepper, Proscuitto, cheese, garlic and egg yolk. Shape into a 2 1/2 x 10-inch loaf. Roll in bread crumbs to coat evenly. Heat butter and oil in large heavy skillet or oval casserole with cover over medium heat. Add loaf and brown on all sides, turning carefully. Add wine; cook over high heat until sauce is reduced by one half. Strain mushrooms through sieve lined with paper towel, reserving liquid. Chop mushrooms; return to pan. Reduce heat to medium. Combine tomato paste with reserved mushroom liquid; add to sauce. Cover and simmer 1 hour, turning meat frequently. Partially uncover pan for final 30 minutes. Remove meat from pan. To serve, pour small amount of sauce on serving platter. Overlap thin meat slices; pour remaining sauce over meat.

Wine Suggestions -
Red: Italian; *Barbaresco*
Red: French; *Crozes Hermitage*

ROBERT J. WHITE, M.D., PH.D.

BEEF CASSEROLE

Servings: 6

1   lb. ground beef

1   (8-oz.) can tomato sauce

2   (4-oz.) cans mushrooms, drained (optional)

1   clove garlic, crushed

1   (3-oz.) pkg. cream cheese, softened

1   cup sour cream

6   green onions, chopped

1   cup shredded Cheddar cheese

1   (8-oz.) pkg. egg noodles, cooked and drained

❖ *P*reheat oven to 350 degrees. Brown ground beef in skillet; drain. Stir in tomato sauce,mushrooms and garlic; simmer 20 minutes. Combine cream cheese, sour cream and green onions. In 2-quart casserole, layer 1/2 noodles, 1/2 beef, 1/2 cheese mixture, 1/2 Cheddar cheese; repeat. Bake at 350 degrees for 20 minutes or until hot and bubbly.

Wine Suggestions -
Red: French; *Moulin A Vent*
Red: California; Ridge Zinfandel

World-renowned neurosurgeon

ROAST SHOULDER
of VEAL

Servings: 6-8

1   (4 1/2 lb.) boneless shoulder of veal

1   clove garlic, cut into thin slivers

1/3   cup Dijon mustard

1   teaspoon dried thyme
    Pepper, to taste

7   strips bacon

1/2   cup butter, softened

3/4   cup dry white wine

❖ *P*reheat oven to 350 degrees. Cut small slits in roast; insert garlic slivers. Place roast in shallow pan; rub all over with mustard. Sprinkle with thyme and pepper. Wrap bacon around roast. Spread butter over bacon. Pour wine into pan. Bake at 350 degrees 30 minutes per pound or until juice runs clear, basting frequently. Serve pan juices with meat.

Wine Suggestions -
Red: California; *Clos du Bois;* Merlot
White: California; *Matanzas Creek;* Sauvignon Blanc
Red: French; *St. Emilion Ch. Belair*

VEAL MEDALLIONS
in
MUSTARD-CREAM
SAUCE

Servings: 4-6

4	tablespoons butter
2	tablespoons oil
4	green onions, chopped
1³/4	lbs. veal medallions
	Pepper, to taste
1/3	cup dry white wine
3	tablespoons Dijon mustard
1/2	cup whipping cream
1	large tomato, peeled, seeded and chopped
	Chopped fresh parsley
1	teaspoon fresh thyme, minced (1/2 teaspoon dried thyme)

❖ *M*elt butter and oil in large skillet. Add green onions and cook for 5 minutes over low heat. Add veal and pepper to taste. Increase heat and cook 1 minute per side. Remove veal and keep warm. Add wine to skillet and bring to a boil. Cook until mixture is reduced to 1/4 cup. Whisk in mustard and cream; boil for 2 minutes. Place veal on serving dish. Spoon sauce over veal. Garnish with tomatoes and parsley. Sprinkle with thyme.

Wine Suggestions -
White: French; *Sancerre*
White: California; *Robert Mondavi;* Chardonnay
Red: California; *Francisian;* Cabernet Sauvignon

BERNIE KOSAR

VEAL and SAUSAGE
SCAPARELLA

Servings: 4

2	tablespoons olive oil
2	cloves garlic
1	lb. veal, thinly sliced and cut into 2-inch pieces
1	lb. Italian sausage, cut into bite-sized pieces
1	large green pepper, seeded and cubed
1/2	cup sliced fresh mushrooms
1	medium onion, chopped
1/8	chopped pepperoncini
1/2	teaspoon dried oregano
1/2	teaspoon dried basil
1/2	teaspoon dried thyme
1/2	teaspoon salt
1/2	teaspoon pepper
1/4	cup dry white wine

❖ *H*eat oil in skillet over medium heat. Add garlic and saute 1 to 2 minutes. Add veal and sausage. Cook on one side until lightly browned. Turn meat and add green pepper, mushrooms, onion, pepperoncini, oregano, basil, thyme, salt and pepper. Cover and simmer 20 minutes. Add wine and cook uncovered 10 minutes. Serve over rice or pasta with green salad.

Wine Suggestions -
Red: French; Julienas
Red: California; *Bouchaide;* Pinot Noir

Former Quarterback for the Cleveland Browns

COMPANY VEAL

Servings: 4

1½   lbs. veal sirloin, cut into cubes

Marinade

4   tablespoons vegetable oil

4   tablespoons lemon juice

1   teaspoon salt

1   teaspoon paprika

½   teaspoon ground nutmeg

1   teaspoon prepared mustard

2   cloves garlic, minced

½   cup all-purpose flour

4   tablespoons butter

1⅓   cups chicken broth

1   green pepper, cut into strips

2   cups sliced fresh mushrooms

2   medium onions, sliced and
    separated into rings

❖ MARINADE: Place veal in large
bowl. Combine all marinade ingredients;
pour over veal. Marinate 30 minutes.

Preheat oven to 350 degrees.
Remove veal, reserving marinade. Dredge
veal in flour. In large skillet, saute veal in
butter. Place in 3-quart casserole. Combine
reserved marinade, chicken broth, green
pepper, mushrooms and onions; pour over
veal. Cover and bake at 350 degrees for 60
minutes. Remove cover and bake additional
15 to 20 minutes.

Wine Suggestions:
Red: French; *Croles Hermitage*
Red: California; *Saintsbury;* Pinot Noir
White: French; *Puligny Montrachet*

HERB GARDEN LAMB

Servings: 6-8

1 (8 lb.) leg of lamb

Marinade

    Rind of 4 lemons

    Juice of 4 lemons

6 cloves garlic, chopped

1 tablespoon salt

1 tablespoon pepper

½ cup chopped fresh parsley

2 teaspoons chopped fresh rosemary

1 teaspoon fresh thyme

½ cup olive oil

Sauce

1 cup chopped green onions

2 tablespoons butter

1 tablespoon flour

1½ cups chicken stock

1 tablespoon sugar

½ cup whipping cream

2 tablespoons Dijon mustard

1 tablespoon flour

❖ *P*lace lamb in large bowl. Combine all marinade ingredients; pour over lamb. Marinate, covered, in refrigerator overnight. Heat oven to 375 degrees. Roast lamb uncovered 20 minutes per pound or until pink in center. Baste frequently.

SAUCE: Saute green onions in butter. Stir in flour. Add chicken stock and sugar; bring to a boil. Add cream and mustard. Simmer over high heat until sauce is slightly reduced. Slice lamb and serve with sauce.

SERVING SUGGESTION: Reserve greens from onions. Wilt and place on platter as a bed for sliced lamb.

Wine Suggestions -
Red: French; *CH. Ducru Beaucaillou*
Red: California; *Robert Mondavi*; Cabernet Sauvignon
White: California; *Grgich Hills;* Chardonnay

FRUITED LAMB CURRY

Servings: 10

2 tablespoons butter

4 lbs. boneless lamb, all fat removed, cut into 1-inch chunks

4 medium onions, chopped

2 teaspoons minced garlic

1/4 cup curry powder

1/2 teaspoon salt

1 (28-oz.) can tomatoes, undrained and chopped

1 (6-oz.) can tomato paste

4 cups water

1 (16-oz.) can chick peas, drained

1 cup dried apricots

1 cup raisins

❖ *M*elt butter in Dutch oven over medium-high heat. Add half of lamb. Cook, stirring for 4 minutes or until meat loses its pink color. Remove lamb. Repeat with remaining lamb. Pour off all but 1/4 cup of drippings. Add onions and garlic. Cook for 4 minutes or until lightly browned. Stir in curry and salt. Reduce heat to low and cook 3 minutes. Add tomatoes, tomato paste, water and lamb. Cover and bring to a simmer over medium heat for 40 minutes. Stir in chick peas, apricots and raisins. Simmer uncovered for 20 minutes or until meat is tender.

Wine Suggestions -
Red: French; *Chiroubles* or *Beaujolais Villages*
Red: California; *Beringer;* Gamay

LAMB CHOPS PROVENÇAL

Servings: 4

4 (8-oz.) loin lamb chops, fat removed

Salt and pepper

1 tablespoon olive oil

2 teaspoons chopped fresh rosemary (1 teaspoon dried)

4 springs fresh thyme (1 teaspoon dried thyme)

2 tablespoons chopped onion

2 teaspoons minced garlic

1 tablespoon red wine vinegar

2 cups fresh tomatoes, seeded and cut into 1/2-inch cubes

1 bay leaf (if desired)

1/4 cup pitted black olives

1/4 cup pitted green olives

1/4 cup fresh basil or parsley

❖ *S*prinkle lamb chops with salt and pepper. In heavy skillet, brown lamb chops in olive oil on one side, about 5 minutes. Turn and sprinkle with rosemary and thyme. Cook 5 minutes for rare, longer for medium or well done. Remove chops to warm platter. Pour off all but 1 tablespoon fat from skillet. Saute onion and garlic until wilted. Add vinegar, tomatoes, bay leaf and olives. Add salt and pepper, to taste. Simmer 5 minutes. Remove bay leaf and pour mixture over chops. Garnish with basil or parsley.

Wine Suggestions -
Red: French; *Hermitage*
Red: California; *Franciscan Meritage;* Cabernet Sauvignon

MEDALLIONS of PORK

Servings: 6

1/2	teaspoon salt
2 1/2	lb. boneless pork loin, cut into 3/4 to 1-inch slices
1	tablespoon all-purpose flour
6	tablespoons brandy
1 1/2	cups whipping cream
1 1/2	cups chicken stock
	Salt and freshly ground pepper
1 1/2	cups chopped walnuts

❖ *S*prinkle salt in bottom of hot, sterilized 1 quart wide-mouthed canning jar. Layer pork slices in jar leaving space (do not pack). Immediately wipe rim using towel dipped in hot water. Place lid on jar; seal tightly. Set jar in large pot. Cover with boiling water by at least 1 inch Cover pot and boil gently for 3 1/2 hours. Cool.

Melt 2 to 3 teaspoons fat from jar over medium heat. Add pork and brown well on both sides. Remove. Whisk flour into skillet and cook 3 minutes. Stir in brandy and bring to a boil. Blend in cream and stock and boil until thickened. Season with salt and pepper. Stir in walnuts. Spoon over pork. Serve immediately.

Wine Suggestions -
Red: Australian; *Michelton Vineyards Cabernet-Merlot*
White: California; *William Hill*; Chardonnay

BRIAN BRENNAN

STUFFED PORK CHOPS

Servings: 6

6	pork loin chops, 1 1/2-inches thick

Stuffing

2	tablespoons raisins
1/2	cup chopped apples
1 1/2	cups toasted bread crumbs
1/2	cup shredded sharp Cheddar cheese
2	tablespoons orange juice
2	tablespoons melted butter
1/4	teaspoon salt
1/8	teaspoon cinnamon

❖ *P*reheat oven to 350 degrees. Cut deep pocket in fat side of pork chops. Combine stuffing ingredients. Gently stuff each pork chop. Place in shallow baking dish. Bake at 350 degrees for 1 1/2 hours. Cover with foil during last 15 minutes.

Wine Suggestions -
White: Alsatian; Gewürztraminer
White: German; *Rhinegau;* Spatlese
White: California; Johannisberg Riesling

Former Receiver for the Cleveland Browns

George Voinovich

PORK CHOPS

with

APPLES

Servings: 8

- 8 loin pork chops
  Salt and pepper to taste
- 1/2 cup apple juice or cider
- 3 tablespoons ketchup
- 1/2 cup soy sauce
- 1/2 cup firmly packed brown sugar
- 2 tablespoons cornstarch
- 1/2 teaspoon ground ginger
- 2 Golden Delicious apples, cored and cut into rings

❖ *P*reheat oven to 350 degrees. Place pork chops in single layer in roasting pan. Sprinkle with salt and pepper. Bake at 350 degrees for 30 minutes.

In medium saucepan, combine apple juice, ketchup, soy sauce, brown sugar, cornstarch and ginger. Cook over medium heat until thickened. Spoon juice from roasting pan to thin sauce. Place apple slice on each pork chop. Spoon sauce over chops. Bake additional 30 minutes, basting frequently. Governor Voinovich likes this served with rice and broccoli.

Wine Suggestions -
White: Alsatian; Riesling
White: German; *Rhinegau;* Spatlese

Former Mayor of Cleveland, 1991 Governor of Ohio

PORK TENDERLOIN with

MARMALADE SAUCE

Servings: 6

- 3 tablespoons whole grain mustard
- 2 cloves garlic, minced
- 1 teaspoon dried rosemary, crushed
  Freshly ground black pepper
- 2 (3/4 lb.) pork tenderloins, trimmed

Sauce
- 1/2 cup orange marmalade
- 1/2 cup chicken stock
- 1 teaspoon freshly grated ginger
- 1 tablespoon soy sauce
- 1-2 teaspoons cornstarch
- 1/2-1 teaspoon water

❖ *P*reheat oven to 400 degrees. In small bowl, combine mustard, garlic, rosemary and pepper. Completely cover each tenderloin with mustard mixture. Form roast of uniform thickness and tie with string. Place on rack in roasting pan. Bake at 400 degrees for 50 to 60 minutes or until internal temperature is 160 degrees.

SAUCE: Combine marmalade, stock, ginger and soy sauce in small saucepan. Heat to boiling. Mix cornstarch with water to form a thick paste; add to sauce. Stir until sauce thickens. Serve pork with sauce on the side.

Wine Suggestions -
White: California; *Kendall Jackson;* Chardonnay
Red: French; *Beaujolais Villages*
White: German; *Steinberger;* Spatlese

PORK en CROUTE

Servings: 4

1	(1-lb.) pork tenderloin

Filling:

1/2	lb. fresh mushrooms, finely chopped
1/4	cup sliced green onions
2	tablespoons butter
1	tablespoon dry sherry
1	teaspoon lemon juice
1	tablespoon dry bread crumbs
1/4	teaspoon salt
1/4	teaspoon dried basil

Crust

1	sheet frozen puff pastry, thawed
1	egg, beaten
1	tablespoon water

❖ *P*reheat oven to 350 degrees. Remove cartilage or fat from tenderloin. Tuck ends of tenderloin under to form an even thickness of meat. Tie with string. Insert meat thermometer. Roast at 350 degrees for 40 minutes or until internal temperature reaches 165 degrees. Remove from oven; place on rack. Cover tightly with foil; do not allow the meat to cool completely.

While meat is cooking, saute onions and mushrooms in butter. Stir in sherry and lemon juice. Cook, stirring until liquid evaporates. Remove from heat. Stir in bread crumbs, salt and basil. Remove from heat.

Preheat oven to 425 degrees. Grease 15 x 10-inch jelly roll pan. Unfold pastry. Place roast on pastry. Cut pastry allowing 1″ overlap on top and enough pastry on sides to fold under. Return meat to rack and spread center of pastry with mushroom mixture. Place meat on mushroom mixture, rounded side down. Pull pastry firmly together across meat; folding end flaps last. Seal edges with beaten egg. Place seam side down on prepared pan. Combine egg and water; brush all over pastry with beaten egg. Prick in several places with fork. Bake at 425 degrees for 25 minutes or until crust is golden.

Wine Suggestions -
Red: French; *St. Emilion;* Bordeaux
Red: California; *Clos du Bois;* Merlot
White: German; *Schloss Volrads Rheingau;* Riesling

KENTUCKY ROAST PORK

Servings: 6

2/3 cup Dijon mustard

1/3 cup firmly packed brown sugar

1 (3 1/2 lb.) boneless pork loin

2 tablespoons vegetable oil

Glaze

1/2 cup bourbon

1/4 teaspoon salt

1/2 teaspoon dried thyme

1/4 teaspoon dried sage

3 Granny Smith apples, peeled, cored and cut into eighths

4 teaspoons cornstarch

1 cup half-and-half

2 cups beef broth

Cooked noodles

❖ *P*reheat oven to 375 degrees. Combine mustard and brown sugar; spread completely over pork. Heat oil in oven-proof baking dish large enough to hold meat. Brown roast slowly being careful not to burn sugar. Remove meat to platter. Spoon off fat from pan. Add bourbon, salt, thyme and sage to pan. Stir over medium heat to loosen particles in pan. Return meat to pan. Cover and bake at 375 degrees for 1 hour and 20 minutes or until internal temperature is 160 degrees. Remove from oven. Skim off excess fat. Add apples. Bake for additional 20 minutes or until internal temperature is 170 degrees. Remove meat and apples to a platter. Combine cornstarch and half-and-half. Stir into meat drippings. Add beef broth. Cook over high heat until mixture thickens. Serve slices of pork and apples with noodles. Pass sauce.

Wine Suggestions -
Red: French; *Chateauneuf du Pape*
Red: California; *Jaeger Vineyards*; Merlot

BARBECUED
PORK LOIN

Servings: 8

Marinade

- 1/2 cup firmly packed brown sugar
- 1/2 cup barbecue sauce with mild garlic flavor
- 1/2 cup dry vermouth or water
- 1/4 cup soy sauce
- 1/4 cup wine vinegar
- 1/8 teaspoon dried ginger

- 5 lb. boneless pork loin
- 1 teaspoon cornstarch

❖ Combine all marinade ingredients until well blended; pour over meat. Cover; refrigerate 6 hours or overnight.

Preheat oven to 425 degrees. Remove meat from marinade; reserve marinade. Reduce oven temperature to 325 degrees. Bake at 325 degrees for 1 1/2 hours or until internal temperature is 160 degrees. Baste frequently while cooking. Allow meat to set for 10 to 15 minutes before slicing

Combine 2 cups reserved marinade with cornstarch; heat until thickened.

Wine Suggestions -
White: Alsace; Gewürztraminer
Red: French; *Chiroubles*
Red: California; Zinfandel

PORK ROAST CASSIS

Servings: 8-10

- 4-5 lb. boneless pork roast

Marinade:

- 1/2 cup soy sauce
- 1/2 cup sherry
- 2 cloves garlic, minced
- 1 tablespoon dry mustard
- 1 teaspoon ground ginger
- 1 teaspoon dried thyme, crushed

Sauce

- 1 (10-oz.) jar currant jelly
- 2 tablespoons Creme de Cassis liqueur
- 3 tablespoons sherry
- 1 tablespoon soy sauce
- 1 1/2 teaspoons cornstarch

❖ MARINADE: Combine all marinade ingredients. Pour marinade over roast in plastic bag. Seal bag; refrigerate 24 hours.

Preheat oven to 325 degrees. Remove meat from marinade; roast for 2 1/2 to 3 hours or until internal temperature is 160 degrees.

SAUCE: Heat currant jelly until melted. Dissolve cornstarch in soy sauce. Add Cassis, sherry and soy sauce. Heat until sauce is slightly thickened. Serve over pork roast.

VARIATION: Add dried currants to sauce.

Wine Suggestions -
Red: California; *Johnson-Turnbull;* Cabernet Sauvignon
White: German; *Raunthaler Baiken Rheingau*

PORK LOIN
NEW ORLEANS

Servings: 8

1/2   **cup pitted prunes**

1/2   **cup dried apricots**

1   **cup bourbon**

1 1/2   **cups fresh bread crumbs**

3/4   **cup pecans, finely chopped**

2   **small onions, minced**

1   **teaspoon dried sage**

1   **tablespoon dried rosemary**

1   **large egg, lightly beaten**

4   **lb. boneless rolled pork loin**

1/4   **cup Dijon mustard**

1/2   **cup firmly packed brown sugar**
     Salt and pepper

1   **cup Chablis (or any dry white wine)**

1   **(16-oz.) can beef or chicken broth**

2   **bay leaves**

❖ *P*reheat oven to 425 degrees. In small saucepan, simmer prunes and apricots in 1/2 cup bourbon for 10 minutes. Remove from heat. Transfer to a large bowl. Add bread crumbs, pecans, onions, sage and rosemary. Add egg in small amounts just until stuffing holds together. Untie pork; gently pack with stuffing. Retie the roast and place in 11 x 13-inch roasting pan. Spread mustard over pork. Carefully pat brown sugar over mustard. Season with salt and pepper. Pour 1/2 cup bourbon, wine and broth around the pork. Add bay leaves. Cover and roast at 425 degrees or until internal temperature is 160 degrees. Baste occasionally with pan juices. Add water if liquid evaporates too rapidly. Allow pork to rest 5 to 10 minutes before slicing. Spoon degreased pan juices over pork, if desired.

Wine Suggestions -
White: German; *Von Simmern* Spatlese Rheingau
White: Ohio; *DeBonne Vineyards;* Johannisberg Riesling
Red: French; *Beaujolais Villages*

STUFFED TURKEY
BREAST
FLORENTINE

Servings: 8-10

Stuffing

2	garlic cloves
1	onion, chopped
2	tablespoons vegetable oil
2	cups fresh mushrooms, chopped
1¹/₂	cups cooked spinach, drained and chopped
1	red pepper, seeded and chopped
1	green pepper, seeded and chopped
1	carrot, shredded
1	cup shredded Mozzarella cheese
¹/₂	cup fresh bread crumbs
	Freshly ground black pepper
2	large eggs, beaten
¹/₂	teaspoon dried thyme
1	(6 lb.) boneless turkey breast with skin
2¹/₂	tablespoons honey
2¹/₂	tablespoons Dijon mustard

❖ STUFFING: Saute onion and garlic in oil until translucent. Stir in mushrooms, spinach, red and green peppers and carrot. Saute until moisture evaporates, about 3 to 4 minutes. Cool. Add cheese, bread crumbs, pepper, eggs, and thyme.

Place turkey breast skin side down. Open breast so turkey lies flat; butterfly thick portion of breast, turning pieces to outside. Cover with wax paper or plastic wrap and pound slightly to make uniform thickness. Spoon stuffing in a 2 to 3-inch strip down center of breast. Turn in the sides of breast and roll, securing with toothpicks or small skewers.

Preheat oven to 425 degrees. Place in large greased pan and cover with greased foil. Seal tightly. Bake at 425 degrees for 40 minutes. Reduce temperature to 350 degrees and remove foil. Combine honey and mustard. Baste turkey with honey mixture. Bake for 30 minutes. Allow turkey to set 10 to 15 minutes before slicing

Wine Suggestions -
Red: Italian; *Brunelo de Montalcino*
Red: French; *Hermitage*
White: California; *Z.D. Vineyards,* Chardonnay

TAMERA WHITE

CHICKEN with LIME BUTTER

Servings: 4-6

3   **whole chicken breasts, boned, skinned and halved**

1/2   **teaspoon salt**

1/2   **teaspoon pepper**

1/3   **cup vegetable oil**
      Juice of 1 lime

1/2   **cup butter**

1   **teaspoon minced chives**

1/2   **teaspoon dill**

❖ Sprinkle chicken with salt and pepper. Heat oil in large skillet over medium heat. Saute chicken until light brown, about 3 minutes per side. Cover; reduce heat to low. Cook 10 minutes or until chicken is tender. Remove chicken to serving platter. Drain oil from skillet. Add lime juice. Cook over low heat until juice begins to boil, about 1 minute. Add butter, 1 tablespoon at a time, until butter becomes opaque and forms a thick sauce. Remove from heat. Stir in chives and dill. Spoon sauce over chicken. Serve immediately.

Wine Suggestions -
White: French: Sancerre
White: California: *Kistler;* Chardonnay

1991 First Lady of Cleveland

CHICKEN SALTIMBOCCA

Servings: 6

3   **whole chicken breasts, boned and skinned**

3   **thin slices boiled ham**

3   **thin slices Mozzarella cheese**

1   **medium tomato, seeded, skinned and chopped**

1/2   **teaspoon poultry seasoning**

1/3   **cup fine Italian bread crumbs**

2   **tablespoons Parmesan cheese**

2   **tablespoons chopped fresh parsley**

4   **tablespoons butter, melted**

❖ Preheat oven to 350 degrees. Cover chicken breasts with plastic wrap and pound lightly until even thickness. Place a slice of ham and cheese, trimmed to fit, on each breast. Top with tomato and dash of poultry seasoning. Tuck in sides; roll up jelly roll style pressing to seal. Secure with toothpicks. Combine bread crumbs, Parmesan cheese and parsley. Dip chicken in butter; coat with bread crumbs. Place in shallow baking pan. Bake at 350 degrees for 40 to 45 minutes. Remove toothpicks; cut in half to serve.

Wine Suggestions -
White: California; *Flora Springs;* Sauvignon Blanc
White: Italian; Pinot Grigio
Red: California; *Ravenswood;* Zinfandel

CHAMPAGNE CHICKEN

Servings: 4-6

4   whole chicken breasts, halved, boned and skinned

Salt and pepper

Flour

2   tablespoons butter

2   tablespoons oil

1/2   lb. fresh mushrooms, sliced

2   tablespoons minced shallots

3   tablespoons Madeira wine

1/2   cup plus 2 tablespoons Brut Champagne

1   cup chicken stock

1/2   cup whipping cream

1/4   cup butter, softened

❖ *P*reheat oven to 425 degrees. Grease baking sheet. Pound chicken between sheets of wax paper until flattened to 1/2-inch. Season with salt and pepper; dredge in flour. Heat 2 tablespoons butter and oil in large skillet over medium-high heat; add chicken. Cook until golden brown, about 3 minutes on each side. Add mushrooms and shallots and cook for 1 to 2 minutes. Pour off grease. Add Madeira. Using long match, ignite Madeira; allow flames to die. Add 1/2 cup champagne and chicken stock; bring to simmer. Bring liquid in skillet to a boil. Reduce liquid by two-thirds. Add cream and boil until slightly thickened. Adjust seasoning. Transfer chicken to prepared baking sheet; reduce heat. Bake chicken at 425 degrees until springy to the touch, about 4 minutes. Meanwhile add remaining 2 tablespoons champagne to sauce. Swirl in softened butter, 1 tablespoon at a time. Spoon sauce over chicken to serve.

Wine Suggestions -
White: California; *Roederer Estate;* Champagne Brut
Red: French; Pouilly Fuisse

The Westside Market

CHICKEN with BRIE and WALNUTS

Servings: 4-6

4   whole chicken breasts, halved, boned and skinned

$1/8$ teaspoon pepper

$1/2$ cup all-purpose flour

$1/2$ cup vegetable oil

1   cup dry vermouth or dry white wine

$1^1/2$ teaspoons chicken base

$1/2$ cup butter

$1/2$ lb. fresh mushrooms, quartered

1   cup walnut halves

10   oz. Brie cheese, sliced, rind removed

❖ Cover chicken breasts with plastic wrap and pound lightly until $1/4$-inch thick. Sprinkle with pepper. Dredge chicken in flour to coat all sides; shake off excess. In large skillet, heat oil over medium heat. Saute chicken about 10 minutes or until light brown. Remove chicken from pan and keep warm. Drain oil from pan. Combine vermouth and chicken base; set aside. Saute mushrooms and walnuts in butter 2 minutes. Stir in vermouth and Brie. Simmer over low heat until slightly thickened. Arrange chicken on heated platter. Pour sauce over chicken to serve.

Wine Suggestions -
White: California; *Saintsbury;* Chardonnay
White: French; Pouilly Fuisse
Red: California; *Beringer;* Pinot Noir or Gamay

STUFFED CHICKEN BREASTS en CROUTE

Servings: 4

2   whole chicken breasts, boned, skinned and split

2   tablespoons minced garlic

1   tablespoon butter

2   oz. goat cheese, room temperature

7-8   sun-dried tomatoes marinated in oil, cut into small pieces

3   oz. frozen spinach, thawed and drained

2   sheets puff pastry, thawed

1   egg, beaten

1   tablespoon water

❖ Preheat oven to 400 degrees. In medium skillet, saute chicken and garlic in butter until light brown. In small bowl, mash goat cheese, tomatoes and spinach until well combined. Spread $1/4$ of mixture on each chicken breast. Cut puff pastry sheets in half. Place chicken breast, spinach side down onto pastry. Wrap pastry around chicken. Cut off excess pastry and crimp edges to seal. Place on cookie sheet seam side down. If desired, decorate each pastry with excess pastry. Combine egg and water. Brush each pastry with egg wash. Cut a small slit in top of each pastry for steam to escape. Bake at 400 for 35 minutes or until golden brown.

Wine Suggestions -
White: French; Graves; *CH. Graville Lacoste*
White: California; *Burgess;* Chardonnay

DAY AHEAD CHICKEN

Servings: 4-6

3-4	whole chicken breasts, skinned, halved and boned
1/2	cup honey
1/2	cup Dijon mustard
1	tablespoon curry powder
2	tablespoons soy sauce

❖ *P*lace chicken in baking dish. Chicken should fit snugly. Combine honey, mustard, curry and soy sauce. Pour over chicken. Cover tightly with foil. Refrigerate for several hours or overnight. Heat oven to 350 degrees. Bake, covered, for 40 minutes. Uncover; baste and bake additional 10 minutes. Spoon sauce over chicken to serve.

Wine Suggestions -
White: California; Johannisberg Riesling
White: California; *Buehler;* White Zinfandel

FRENCH STYLE CHICKEN with THREE MUSTARDS

Servings: 4

2	whole chicken breasts, skinned, boned and cut into bite-size pieces
1/8	teaspoon paprika
	Dash salt
	Dash pepper
1	tablespoon vegetable oil
1	tablespoon unsalted butter
1/2	cup dry vermouth
1	tablespoon Dijon mustard
1	tablespoon whole grain mustard
1	teaspoon dry mustard
1	cup whipping cream

❖ *S*prinkle chicken with paprika, salt and pepper. Heat 1 tablespoon each of oil and butter in skillet. Cook 1/2 of chicken until golden brown. Remove to platter and repeat for remaining chicken. Add vermouth to skillet and bring to a boil, scraping sides of pan. Whisk in Dijon, whole grain and dry mustard and cream. Reduce mixture until it is thick enough to coat back of spoon. Return chicken to sauce and heat through. Serve over rice or noodles.

Wine Suggestions -
White: French; *Chassagne Montrachet*
White: California; *Arrowwood Vineyards;* Chardonnay
Rose: French; *Tavel*

CHICKEN OLIVADA

Servings: 6-8

2 cloves garlic, minced
1/2 teaspoon salt
1/2 teaspoon paprika
1/2 teaspoon cayenne pepper
2 teaspoons lemon juice
1/2 cup olive oil
1/4 cup vegetable oil
3 lbs. chicken breasts, skinned and boned
Black Olivada paste*

❖ *I*n a medium bowl, combine garlic, salt, paprika and cayenne pepper. Mash with back of spoon until well combined. Let stand 5 minutes. Whisk in lemon juice, olive oil and vegetable oil. Place chicken between wax paper, pound until flattened. Add chicken to marinade and toss until chicken is well coated. Marinate at room temperature for 2 hours. Prepare grill. Remove chicken from marinade. Spread both sides of chicken with thin layer of olivada paste. Grill for 3-5 minutes or until chicken is just cooked through.

Olivada paste is available at specialty stores. It is a paste made from ripe Italian olives.

Wine Suggestions -
White: Italy; *Terre di Tufo*
White: California; *Mondavi Reserve;* Sauvignon Blanc

HURRY CURRY CHICKEN

Servings: 4-6

1 tablespoons butter or margarine
2 tablespoons vegetable oil
4 whole chicken breasts, halved, skinned and boned
1 medium onion, chopped
3 cloves garlic, minced
3 tablespoons curry powder
2/3 cup diced apple
1/2 cup dried apricots
1/2 cup raisins
1 (13-oz.) can chicken broth
1/2 cup unsalted cashews
Freshly cooked rice

❖ *M*elt butter and oil in skillet over medium heat. Saute chicken until lightly browned. Transfer to a plate. Add onion and garlic; saute 6 minutes. Stir in curry powder. Return chicken to skillet. Stir in apples, apricots and raisins. Add broth to just cover chicken. Cover and cook 10 minutes. Remove chicken to warm platter. Simmer fruit mixture until thickened. Add cashews. Spoon sauce over chicken, serve with rice.

Wine Suggestions -
White: German; *Piesporter Goldtropchen*
White: California; *William Hill Vineyards;* White Riesling

CRUNCHY PECAN COATED CHICKEN

Servings: 2-4

1   cup pecans
1/4   cup dry bread crumbs
2   tablespoons Cajun seasoning
2   whole chicken breasts, halved, boned and skinned
2   eggs, slightly beaten
  Oil

❖ *P*rocess pecans, bread crumbs and seasoning in food processor until consistency of coarse cornmeal. Dip chicken in egg; dredge in crumb mixture. Refrigerate 30 minutes. Heat 1/4-inch oil in heavy skillet; cook chicken until done. Coating will be very dark brown or black.

Wine Suggestions -
Red: California; *Joseph Swan;* Zinfandel
White: German; *Rudesheime Berg Rotland;* Riesling Spatlese

BOB HOPE

FAVORITE CHICKEN HASH

Servings: 4

2   tablespoons butter
2   whole chicken breasts, boned, broiled and cut into strips
2   strips bacon, fried, drained and crumbled
1/2   small onion, chopped
1/2   teaspoon lemon juice
  Salt and pepper, to taste
2   tablespoons sour cream
1   teaspoon dry sherry

❖ *M*elt butter in large saucepan. Add chicken, bacon, onion, lemon juice, salt and pepper. Cook until heated through. Stir in sour cream and sherry. Cook until just heated through.

Wine Suggestions -
White: French; Pouilly Fuisse
White: California; *Simi Reserve;* Chardonnay
Red: California; *Clos Du Bois;* Merlot

Native Clevelander, America's Entertainment Ambassador

TORTILLAS SANTA FE

Servings: 2-4 Entree,
8-10 as an Appetizer

1/2 cup vegetable oil

6 (8-inch) flour tortillas

1 cup sour cream

1/2 teaspoon salt

1/2 teaspoon pepper

1/2 teaspoon ground cumin

 Chopped fresh cilantro

1/2 teaspoon hot pepper sauce

2 cups shredded Monterey Jack cheese

2 cups shredded Colby cheese

2 1/2 cups shredded boiled chicken

3/4 cup minced green onions

1/2 cup finely shredded lettuce

1/4 cup diced tomato

❖ Preheat oven to 400 degrees. Heat oil in heavy skillet. Fry tortillas until lightly browned and crisp, about 10 seconds on each side. Drain on paper towels. Combine sour cream, salt, pepper, cumin, cilantro and pepper sauce. In medium bowl, combine cheeses. To assemble, place two tortillas on cookie sheet. Top each with 1 tablespoon sour cream mixture, 1/2 cup chicken, 3/4 cup cheese and 2 tablespoons green onion. Top with tortillas. Repeat layers. Top with remaining tortillas. Cover with foil and bake at 400 degrees for 20 to 25 minutes. To serve, spread each with remaining sour cream, garnish with shredded lettuce and tomato.

CORNISH HENS with FRUITED STUFFING

Servings: 4-6

4-6 Cornish game hens, rinsed and patted dry
 Salt

1/3 cup chopped onion

1/3 cup chopped celery

1 tablespoon butter or margarine

1 (16-oz.) can whole cranberry sauce

1 (12-oz.) can fried rice

1 (8-oz.) can crushed pineapple, drained, reserving juice

1 (8-oz.) can apricots, drained and chopped, reserving juice

1 (8-oz.) can water chestnuts, drained and chopped

1/4 teaspoon ground ginger

1/4 cup soy sauce

❖ Preheat oven to 375 degrees. Sprinkle hen cavities with salt. Cook onion and celery in butter until soft. Combine with cranberry sauce, fried rice, pineapple, apricots, water chestnuts and ginger. Lightly spoon into cavities. Tie legs together. Place in shallow baking pan; cover with foil. Bake at 375 degrees for 30 minutes. Uncover hens; combine reserved fruit juices and soy sauce; bake hens an additional hour, basting frequently. Place any remaining stuffing in small casserole and bake at 375 degrees for 45 minutes.

Wine Suggestions -
Red: Alsace; Gewürztraminer
White: California; Johannisberg Riesling

HONEY GLAZED DUCK
with
FRENCH LENTILS

Servings: 4

Lentils

- 2 tablespoons butter
- 1/4 cup finely chopped shallots
- 1 cup dried lentils
- 2 cups water
- Bouquet garni (parsley, bay leaf, thyme and tarragon)
- 1-2 tablespoons quatres epices (3 tablespoons ground white peppercorns, 1 teaspoon cloves, 1/2 teaspoon nutmeg and 1 teaspoon ginger)
- Salt
- Pepper

Duck

- 2 whole duck breasts, skin on, cut in half
- 1/3 cup honey
- 1 tablespoon quatre epices

Sauce

- 1/4 cup port wine
- 1/2 cup beef broth or veal stock
- 1/2 cup mushroom juice (liquid from 8-oz. mushrooms cooked in 1 cup water)
- 1 tablespoon chopped fresh tarragon
- Salt

❖ LENTILS: In medium saucepan, melt butter over medium heat. Add shallots; cook until soft but not brown. Add lentils, water, and bouquet garni. Bring to a boil. Reduce heat to low; skim surface. Add quatre epices, salt and pepper. Cook until lentils are tender, about 30 to 40 minutes. Keep warm.

DUCK: In small saucepan, combine honey and quatre epices. Cook over high heat until honey reaches soft boil stage, about 235 degrees F. Keep warm. Make 4 or 5 horizontal cuts the length of each duck breast through skin but not into meat. Make 4 or 5 cuts vertical cuts. In large skillet over medium-high heat, cook duck, skin side down, until skin is brown. Reduce heat to medium. Cook duck until internal temperature reaches 140 degrees, about 20 minutes. Remove fat from pan during and at end of cooking. Remove duck from pan. Brush skin side with honey mixture. Keep warm.

SAUCE: In skillet in which duck was prepared, cook wine, broth, mushroom juice and tarragon over low heat until mixture is reduced by half. Add salt and pepper to taste.

To serve, arrange lentils on serving platter. Slice duck meat and arrange over lentils. Top with sauce.

Wine Suggestions -
Red: French; *CH. Lynch Bages*
White: California; *Arrowwood*; Merlot
White: California; *Long*; Chardonnay

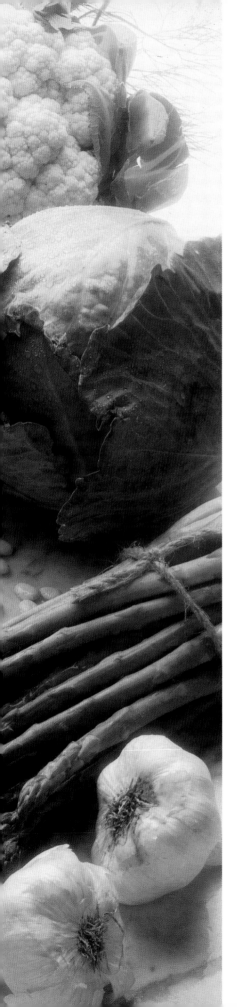

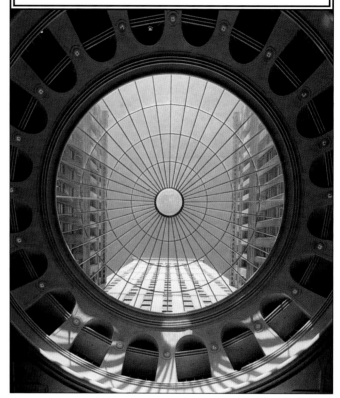

Rice & Vegetables

The Terminal Tower

I n this chapter we invite you to rediscover the pleasures and healthy surprises of natural ingredients. Inspired by creativity and imagination we have a collection of classic recipes with an original twist, that become just a little bit different. We invite you to embellish your meal with these enticing recipes, fit for the connoisseur with distinctive tastes.

ARTICHOKE QUICHE

Servings: 6-8

1   (10-inch) unbaked pie shell
1   egg white, beaten
Filling
3   eggs
1½   cups light cream
1½   cups grated Swiss cheese,
½   teaspoon salt
¼   teaspoon dried thyme, crushed
    Dash cayenne pepper
1   (8½-oz.) can artichoke hearts,
    drained and halved

❖ *P*reheat oven to 375 degrees. Brush 10-inch pie shell with beaten egg white; set aside.

FILLING: In large bowl, combine eggs and light cream; beat well. Stir in cheese, salt, thyme and pepper. Pour into prepared pie shell. Arrange artichokes on top. Bake at 375 degrees for 45 to 60 minutes or until pastry is golden brown and knife inserted into filling comes out clean.

SAUTEED CABBAGE

Servings: 6-8

2   tablespoons vegetable oil
1   small head green cabbage,
    shredded
1   small head red cabbage,
    shredded
1   green pepper, cut into
    julienne strips
1   red pepper, cut into julienne strips
2   tablespoons Cajun seasoning

❖ *H*eat oil in large skillet. Saute cabbage and peppers until crisp-tender. Add Cajun seasoning to taste. Cover and cook 1 minute. Serve immediately.

CURRIED CARROTS

Servings: 6-8

12   medium carrots, peeled and sliced
6   tablespoons butter
1½   tablespoons curry powder
¼   cup lemon juice
2   tablespoons firmly packed brown sugar
Salt and pepper, to taste
Chopped pecans

❖ Cook carrots in water until tender, about 15 to 20 minutes. Drain and return to pan. Stir in butter, curry, lemon juice, brown sugar, salt and pepper to taste. Heat until carrots are glazed, stirring occasionally. Garnish with chopped pecans. Serve immediately.

PECAN GLAZED CARROTS

Servings: 6-8

2-3   lbs. carrots, cooked and mashed (6 cups)
2   eggs, beaten
½   cup firmly packed brown sugar
6   tablespoons butter
¾   teaspoon baking powder
½   teaspoon salt
1   teaspoon cinnamon
¾-1   cup orange juice
1   cup pecan halves
¼   cup firmly packed brown sugar
2   tablespoons butter

❖ Preheat oven to 375 degrees. Butter a 2-quart baking dish. Combine carrots, eggs, ½ cup brown sugar, 6 table-spoons butter, baking powder, salt, cinnamon and orange juice. Mixture should be moist and fluffy. Spread evenly in prepared dish. Arrange pecan halves over top. Sprinkle with remaining brown sugar and dot with 2 tablespoons butter. Bake at 375 degrees for 20 minutes or until heated through.

BROCCOLI SUPREME

Servings: 8-10

3   cups cottage cheese

4   eggs

6   tablespoons butter, softened

2   (10-oz.) pkgs. frozen chopped broccoli, cooked and drained

1   medium onion, finely minced

1   (8-oz.) can whole kernel corn, drained

2^1/$_2$ cups grated Cheddar cheese

^{1}/$_2$ teaspoon salt

^{1}/$_4$ teaspoon pepper

Few drops hot pepper sauce

^{2}/$_3$ cup fresh bread crumbs

❖ *P*reheat oven to 350 degrees. Grease a deep 2 ^{1}/$_2$ quart baking dish. In large bowl, combine cottage cheese, eggs and 4 tablespoons butter. Beat until mixture is smooth and creamy. Fold in broccoli, onion, corn, cheese, salt, pepper and hot pepper sauce. Pour mixture into prepared baking dish. Melt remaining 2 tablespoons butter in saucepan. Add bread crumbs and saute until golden brown. Sprinkle over top of broccoli mixture. Bake at 350 degrees for 1 hour or until mixture is set.

CARROT PUREE

Servings: 6

1   small onion, finely chopped

1   green pepper, seeded and finely chopped

1   lb. fresh or frozen carrots, cooked and drained

2   dashes Tabasco sauce

1   clove garlic

1   teaspoon brown sugar

1   (8-oz.) pkg. cream cheese, softened

Salt and pepper, to taste

^{1}/$_2$ cup grated Cheddar cheese

❖ *P*reheat oven to 350 degrees. Place onion in food processor; process until minced. Add green pepper; process until minced. Add carrots and process mixture until pureed. Add Tabasco, garlic, brown sugar; process until well combined. Add cream cheese, salt and pepper to taste. Process until well combined. Pour into 13 x 9-inch pan. Sprinkle Cheddar cheese over top. Bake at 350 degrees for 40 to 60 minutes or until bubbly.

GRATINEE of CAULIFLOWER

Servings: 6-8

6   tablespoons unsalted butter

4   cloves garlic, minced

4   oz. thinly sliced Prosciutto, cut into thin strips

1   large head cauliflower, broken into florets

2   tablespoons unbleached all-purpose flour

1½ cups whipping cream

    Pinch cayenne pepper

    Salt and pepper, to taste

1½ cups grated Swiss cheese

½   cup chopped fresh parsley

❖ *P*reheat oven to 350 degrees. In large skillet melt butter over medium heat. Saute garlic 2 minutes. Stir in Prosciutto and saute 2 minutes. Add cauliflower and cook 3 to 4 minutes or until cauliflower just begins to lose crispness. Stir in flour and cream; blending well. Season with cayenne pepper, salt and pepper to taste. Heat to boiling. Immediately remove from heat. Pour into a shallow gratin dish. Top with cheese and parsley. Bake at 350 degrees for 20 minutes or until top is lightly browned and bubbling. Serve immediately.

BP America Atrium

EGGPLANT and ZUCCHINI MEDLEY

Servings: 4-6

1   medium eggplant, cut into 1-inch cubes
3   medium zucchini, sliced 1/4-inch thick
1   medium onion, sliced
4   oz. fresh mushrooms, sliced
1   clove garlic, minced
2   tablespoons butter or margarine
1   cup Italian bread crumbs
1   cup grated Romano cheese

❖ *I*n small microwave proof bowl, combine eggplant, zucchini, onion, mushrooms, garlic and butter. Cover with plastic wrap and cook in microwave on high for 15 minutes. Remove from oven. Stir in bread crumbs and cheese. Return to microwave for 10 minutes or until set.

CAPONATA

Servings: 10

1   cup olive oil
1 1/2 lb. eggplant, cubed
2   large green peppers, cut into 1-inch pieces
2   large onions, minced
1   clove garlic, minced
1   (28-oz.) can tomatoes, diced
1/3   cup red wine vinegar
1-2   tablespoons capers, rinsed and drained
2   tablespoons sugar
2   tablespoons tomato paste
2   teaspoons salt
1/2   teaspoon pepper
1/2   cup chopped fresh parsley
1/2   cup pimento stuffed olives, sliced
2   tablespoons dried basil
1 1/2-2 cups pine nuts, sauteed in butter

❖ *I*n large heavy skillet, combine olive oil, eggplant, green peppers, onion, garlic and tomatoes. Cook over medium heat 25 minutes. Add vinegar, capers, sugar, tomato paste, salt, pepper, parsley, olives and basil. Simmer 15 minutes. Stir in pine nuts. May be served cold or at room temperature. Can be refrigerated up to 3 weeks.

ELEGANT GREEN BEANS

Servings: 6

1 (16-oz.) pkg. frozen green beans
1 clove garlic
1 teaspoon seasoned salt
3 tablespoons butter
1/4 cup half-and-half
1 cup sour cream
1 tablespoon all-purpose flour
2 tablespoons grated onion
1 teaspoon seasoned salt
1½ cups shredded cheddar cheese
6 tablespoons butter
2/3 cup bread crumbs.

❖ *P*reheat oven to 350 degrees. Prepare green beans as directed on package with garlic clove and 1 teaspoon seasoned salt. Drain green beans; remove garlic clove. In small saucepan, melt 3 tablespoons butter. Add flour and blend. Stir in half-and-half, sour cream, onion and salt. Combine sauce and beans. Pour into a quiche dish or shallow casserole. Top with cheese. In small saucepan, melt 6 tablespoons butter. Stir in bread crumbs until well combined. Sprinkle over top of cheese. Bake at 350 degrees for 25 minutes.

CINNAMON GREEN BEANS with BACON

Servings: 6

1 tablespoon butter
1/4 cup chopped onion
1/4 teaspoon cinnamon
1½ lbs. fresh green beans, cleaned and trimmed
1/2 cup chicken broth
1/8 teaspoon salt
  Dash freshly ground pepper
2 tablespoons tomato paste
6 slices bacon, fried crisp and crumbled

❖ *M*elt butter in medium saucepan. Saute onion with cinnamon until onion is transparent. Stir in green beans, chicken broth, salt and pepper. Heat to boiling. Reduce heat and simmer 20 minutes or until beans are tender. Gently mix in tomato paste and bacon. Serve immediately.

AMBASSADOR and MRS. MILTON WOLF

MUSHROOM STRUDEL

Servings: 4-6

1   medium onion, coarsley chopped

2½   cups fresh mushrooms, chopped

2   tablespoons butter or margarine

2   tablespoons all-purpose flour

2   tablespoons sherry or Marsala wine

    Salt and pepper, to taste

2   sheets frozen phyllo dough, thawed

2   tablespoons butter or margarine

❖ *P*reheat oven to 400 degrees. Grease or butter a 15 x 10-inch jelly roll pan or cookie sheet. Saute mushrooms and onions in 2 tablespoons butter. Stir in flour, sherry, salt and pepper. Stack 2 sheets phyllo dough on damp towel. Spread filling on phyllo dough starting 2-inches from edge. Fold in half; press edges. Spread 2 tablespoons butter on top of dough. Place on prepared pan. Bake at 400 degrees for 15 minutes or until golden.

Former U.S. Ambassador to Austria

MUSHROOM PARMESAN

Servings: 10-12

1   tablespoon olive oil

1½   lbs. fresh mushrooms, sliced

2   tablespoons chopped fresh parsley

4   cloves garlic, chopped

½   teaspoon dried oregano

¾   cup bread crumbs

4   tablespoons grated Parmesan cheese

    Salt and pepper, to taste

¼   cup extra virgin olive oil

❖ *P*reheat oven to 350 degrees. Brush 2-quart oven-proof casserole with 1 tablespoon olive oil. Add mushrooms. Sprinkle mushrooms with parsley, garlic, oregano, ½ of bread crumbs and 2 tablespoons of Parmesan cheese. Add salt and pepper. Drizzle remaining olive oil over top. Sprinkle remaining bread crumbs and cheese over top. Bake at 350 degrees for 25 minutes or until mushrooms are tender. If mixture is too dry, add ¼ cup water during baking.

ONION PIE

Servings: 4-6

1 cup finely crushed butter crackers
1/4 cup melted butter or margarine
2 cups thinly sliced onions
2 tablespoons butter or margarine
3/4 cup milk
2 eggs, slightly beaten
3/4 teaspoon salt
Dash pepper
Dash paprika
1 cup shredded Cheddar cheese

❖ *P*reheat oven to 350 degrees. Combine cracker crumbs and 1/4 cup melted butter. Press into bottom and up sides of 8" pie plate. Saute onions in 2 tablespoons butter until tender but not browned. Place in prepared pie plate. Combine milk, eggs, salt and pepper. Pour over onions. Sprinkle with paprika and cheese. Bake at 350 degrees for 30 minutes or until knife inserted in center comes out clean. If desired, garnish with additional sauteed onions and parsley.

Sfuzzi's Restaurant

GARLIC MASHED POTATOES

Servings: 4

1 lb. (about 4 medium) potatoes, peeled and halved
1 small head garlic, peeled
4 cups chicken stock
1/2 cup butter
Salt and pepper, to taste
1/2 cup light cream

❖ *P*lace potatoes in sauce pan with garlic and chicken stock. Bring to a boil. Reduce heat. Simmer until potatoes are soft; drain. Gently mash potatoes and garlic with butter, salt, pepper and cream.

POTATOES PATRICIA

Servings: 8

6 medium potatoes
1½ cups creamed cottage cheese
⅓ cup sour cream
¼ cup chopped onions
¼ cup slivered almonds
Salt and pepper, to taste
Melted butter

❖ Cook potatoes in boiling salt water until tender; drain and mash. Heat oven to 350 degrees. Combine potatoes, cottage cheese, sour cream, onions, almonds, salt and pepper. Place mixture in casserole. Brush with butter. Bake for 350 degrees for 30 minutes or until heated through.

TWICE BAKED SWEET POTATOES

Servings: 4

4 sweet potatoes
3 tablespoon butter or margarine
2 tablespoons milk
1 teaspoon salt
⅛ teaspoon pepper
⅓ cup slivered almonds, toasted

❖ Preheat oven to 375 degrees. Bake potatoes 45 to 60 minutes or until tender. Cool slightly. Cut lengthwise slice from top of potato. Carefully scoop out potato, being careful to keep skin intact. Mash potatoes with butter, milk, salt and pepper. Stir in almonds. Carefully spoon mixture into potato shells. Reduce oven temperature to 350 degrees. Bake at 350 degrees for 12 to 15 minutes.

This page has been underwritten through the generosity of PATTY &BROOCK MUNRO.

VEGETABLE MELANGE

Servings: 10-12

5   medium red potatoes, skins on, sliced paper thin
2   large or 3-4 medium tomatoes, diced
1   large onion, chopped
1   green pepper, chopped
1   zucchini, sliced
3/4 cup dry sherry
3   cloves garlic, crushed
3   tablespoons fresh parsley, chopped
1 1/2 teaspoon salt
    Pepper
1/4 cup vegetable oil
    Butter
    Parmesan Cheese

❖ *H*eat oven to 350 degrees. Grease 13 x 9-inch pan. Layer potatoes, tomatoes, onion, green pepper and zucchini in prepared pan. Combine sherry, garlic, parsley, salt, pepper and oil; pour over vegetables. Dot with butter. Cover with foil and bake at 350 degrees for 30 minutes. Remove foil and continue baking 45 minutes. Sprinkle Parmesan cheese over top and bake additional 15 minutes.

SPANAKOPETA
Greek Spinach-Cheese Pie

Yield: 48 pieces

1/2 cup chopped onion
2   tablespoons butter
1   tablespoon water
4   (10-oz.) pkgs. frozen chopped spinach, thawed and drained
1/4 cup chopped fresh parsley
1   tablespoon dried dill weed
1   lb. Feta cheese, crumbled
1   lb. low fat cottage cheese
1   (8-oz.) pkg. cream cheese, softened
4   eggs, slightly beaten
1   lb. phyllo dough, thawed
2   cups butter, melted

❖ *S*aute onion in water and butter until golden. In large bowl, combine onion, spinach, parsley and dill. Add Feta cheese, cottage cheese and cream cheese; blend well. Brush 11 x 17-inch pan with melted butter. Layer 1/2 of phyllo dough in prepared pan, brushing each layer with butter as it is stacked. Spread filling evenly over phyllo. Cover spinach mixture with remaining phyllo dough, brushing each layer with butter as it is stacked. Brush top generously with butter. Refrigerate until firm. (Covered tightly, Spanakopeta may be refrigerated up to two weeks before baking.) Heat oven to 350 degrees. Cut into squares. Bake at 350 degrees for 45 to 60 minutes or until pastry is puffy and golden. May be reheated and refrigerated after baking. Reheat at 350 degrees for 10 to 15 minutes.

SAVORY TOMATOES

Servings: 3

3 large ripe tomatoes
 Salt
 Pepper
 Garlic salt
 Crushed dried oregano
 Mayonnaise
 Freshly grated Parmesan cheese

❖ *P*reheat oven to 450 degrees. Cut tomatoes in half. Cut bottom so the halves sit level on baking sheet. Sprinkle lightly with salt, pepper, garlic salt and oregano. Top each with a dollop of mayonnaise. Sprinkle with Parmesan. Bake at 450 degrees for 10 minutes. Serve piping hot.

VEGETABLE CHILI

Servings: 6-8

2 tablespoons olive oil
2 large onions, chopped
2-3 cloves garlic, minced
1/2 lb. mushrooms, sliced
1 (16-oz.) can red kidney beans, rinsed and drained
1 (28-oz.) can crushed tomatoes with puree
1 (15-oz.) can tomato sauce
3 tablespoons tomato paste
2 tablespoons chili powder
2 small to medium zucchini, sliced
2 red peppers, seeded and chopped
1-2 Jalepeno peppers, seeded and chopped (optional)
 Salt and pepper to taste
1 (10-oz.) pkg. frozen corn
1 (10-oz.) pkg. frozen lima beans

❖ *H*eat oil in Dutch oven. Saute onion and garlic. Add sliced mushrooms and cook until slightly brown. Stir in kidney beans, tomatoes, tomato sauce, tomato paste and chili powder. Heat to boiling. Reduce heat; stir in zucchini, bell pepper, Jalepeno peppers, salt and pepper to taste. Simmer covered about 30 minutes or until vegetables are crisp-tender. Stir in corn and lima beans. Simmer until lima beans are tender, about 10 to 15 minutes. Adjust seasonings.

VEGETABLE
WELLINGTON

Servings: 6

1¼   **cups chopped carrots, blanched and drained**

1¼   **cups chopped zucchini, unpeeled, blanched and drained**

1   **(9x16-inch) sheet puff pastry, thawed**

1   **teaspoon salt**

1   **teaspoon pepper**

1   **teaspoon celery salt**

1½   **cups fresh spinach, washed and dried**

2   **teaspoons lemon juice**

1   **cup fresh tomatoes, diced and well drained**

1   **egg, beaten**

❖ *P*reheat oven to 450 degrees. Cut a 1 x 16-inch strip from puff pastry; set aside. Combine salt, pepper and celery salt. Overlap spinach in a 4" strip down center of 8 x 16" pastry. Arrange carrots over spinach. Sprinkle with 1 teaspoon of combined seasonings and ²/₃ teaspoon lemon juice. Arrange zucchini over carrots. Sprinkle with one third of seasonings and ²/₃ teaspoon lemon juice. Arrange tomatoes over top of zucchini. Sprinkle with remaining seasonings and lemon juice. Fold dough over vegetables, enclosing them completely. Seal edges with beaten egg. Place seam side down on lightly moistened cookie sheet.

Twist reserved pastry strip and lightly press onto top of pastry roll. Brush all over with beaten egg. Chill pastry in refrigerator 15 minutes. Bake at 450 degrees for 20 to 25 minutes or until puffed and golden brown. Check after 10 minutes and cover with parchment paper if browning too quickly.

Chagrin Falls

PEPPERS STUFFED with RICE

Servings: 6

6 red peppers

3/4 cup + 2 tablespoons Arborio rice*

1 tablespoon olive oil

2 cloves garlic, chopped

1/2 teaspoon dried basil

3 anchovy fillets, drained and chopped

4 tablespoons butter

4 tablespoons chopped fresh parsley

❖ *P*reheat oven to 375 degrees. Place whole peppers on cookie sheet. Bake at 375 degrees for 30 minutes. Cut off tops and scrape out seeds. Prepare rice according to package directions; drain. Coat 13 x 9-inch baking dish with olive oil. Cook garlic, basil and anchovies in butter over low heat. Add rice and parsley; stir. Stuff peppers with rice mixture; place in prepared pan. Bake at 375 degrees for 10 minutes.

Arborio rice is an Italian short grain rice.

SAFFRON RICE with PINE NUTS

Servings: 4

1/3 cup pine nuts

2 tablespoons butter

1/3 cup finely chopped onions

1/2 teaspoon minced garlic

1 teaspoon loosely packed saffron threads

1 cup Basmati aromatic long grain rice

1 1/2 cups chicken broth

Salt and pepper

2 tablespoons finely chopped parsley

❖ *P*lace pine nuts in skillet over low heat for 2 to 3 minutes. Shake pan to brown nuts evenly. Pour nuts onto a cool surface. Melt 1 tablespoon butter in saucepan. Add onions; cook briefly. Add garlic and saffron. Stir in rice. Add broth, salt and pepper. Bring to a boil. Cover and simmer 17 minutes. Stir in 1 tablespoon butter, parsley and pine nuts. Serve immediately.

PECAN WILD RICE

Servings: 6-8

1   cup wild rice
1/2   cup butter
1/2   lb. fresh mushrooms, sliced
3   tablespoons minced onion
1   clove garlic, minced
1/2   cup chopped pecans
3   cups chicken broth
    Salt and pepper, to taste

❖ *R*inse wild rice. Cover with boiling water and let stand 1 hour. Preheat oven to 325 degrees. Grease 1 1/2-quart casserole. Melt butter in large saucepan. Add mushrooms, onion and garlic. Cook 5 minutes, stirring often. Add pecans and cook 1 minute. Drain rice and add to mushroom mixture. Add broth, salt and pepper. Pour into prepared pan. Cover and bake at 325 degrees for 1 hour. Uncover and bake additional 20 to 25 minutes.

JOEL GREY

RISO ALFREDO

Servings: 6-8

1   lb. (2 1/2 cups) Arborio rice
2   cups whipping cream
2   cups unsalted butter
1/2   lb. grated Reggiano Italian Parmesan cheese
    Freshly ground pepper

❖ *P*repare rice as directed on package. Cook until al dente. Drain in fine strainer to remove all water. In large saucepan over low heat, reduce cream by 1/3. When reduction is almost complete, stir in 1 cup butter. Stir in rice; remove from heat. Rice will begin to absorb cream. Stir in grated Parmesan cheese. Transfer to a warm bowl. Garnish with additional freshly grated Parmesan. Serve with an Arugula Salad. For a heartier meal, serve with grilled hot Italian sausage. Wine suggestion: a full bodied Chardonnay– Acacia or Mondavi or a French white such as Marquis de la Guiche (Montrachet). For dessert, serve macerated orange slices.

NOTE: If directions are not on rice package, use 1 lb. of rice to 4-5 cups water. Add 1 lb. rice to saucepan. Add 1/2 cup simmering water, stirring constantly. As water is absorbed, continue to add 1/2 cup at a time. Continue until all water is used. Cooking time is approximately 15 to 20 minutes.

Cleveland born Oscar winning actor and dancer

Desserts

A place for contemplation

Beauty isn't always made to last. In this chapter we offer you dazzling ideas that will help make the "final act" a splendid one. Your guests are bound to enjoy the "fruits of your labor" or the pure decadence of a voluptuous chocolate dessert. These dramatic presentations will add the perfect flourish to any occasion.

This section has been underwritten through the generosity of NESTLÉ ENTERPRISES, INC.

WHITE CHOCOLATE CHUNK MACADAMIA COOKIES

Yield: 24 cookies

2/3 cup butter, softened
1/2 cup sugar
1/2 cup firmly packed brown sugar
 1   large egg
1 1/2 cups all-purpose flour
 1   (7-oz.) jar macadamia nuts, coarsely chopped
 6   oz. white chocolate, chopped

❖ *P*reheat oven to 375 degrees. Beat butter, sugar, brown sugar and egg until fluffy. Add flour, nuts and chocolate. Drop by tablespoonfuls onto greased cookie sheets. Bake at 375 degrees for 8 to 10 minutes.

SWEDISH MELTING MOMENTS

Yield: 25 cookies

 1   cup unsalted butter, softened
 6   tablespoons powdered sugar
1 1/4 cups all-purpose flour
1/2 cup cornstarch
1/4 teaspoon almond extract
1/4 teaspoon orange extract
Glaze
 1   cup powdered sugar
 1   tablespoon butter, melted
 1   tablespoon lemon juice
 1   tablespoon orange juice

❖ *C*ream butter and sugar in large bowl. Sift in flour and cornstarch; mix well. Add almond and orange extract. Chill 1 hour. Preheat oven to 350 degrees. Grease cookie sheet. Shape the dough into balls the size of walnuts; place on prepared cookie sheet. Flatten with bottom of wet glass. Bake at 350 degrees for 10 minutes. Cookies will not brown. Carefully remove from pan and spread with glaze.

GLAZE: Combine all glaze ingredients; mix well.

CARAMEL BROWNIES

Yield: 2 dozen

1 (14-oz.) pkg. caramels
1 (2½-oz.) can evaporated milk
1 box German chocolate pudding in mix cake mix
⅔ cup butter or margarine, softened
1 cups chopped walnuts or pecans
1 (12-oz.) pkg. chocolate chips

❖ *P*reheat oven to 350 degrees. Grease 9 x 13-inch pan. Melt caramels with milk in double boiler or microwave. In medium bowl, combine cake mix, butter and nuts; mixture will be thick. Place half of batter in prepared pan. Bake at 350 degrees for 7-8 minutes. Remove from oven; sprinkle with chocolate chips. Pour caramel sauce over chocolate chips and top with remaining batter. Bake at 350 degrees for 18 minutes. Cool; cut into 1-inch squares. Refrigerate after cutting.

This page has been underwritten through the generosity of Julia Sullivan.

PEPPERMINT FUDGE BARS

Yield: 16

2 oz. (2 squares) semi-sweet chocolate
½ cup butter
1 cup sugar
2 eggs, beaten
¼ teaspoon peppermint extract
½ cup all-purpose flour
Pinch salt

Filling
1 tablespoon butter, softened
½ tablespoon cream
½ cup powdered sugar

Glaze
1½ oz. (1½ squares) semi-sweet chocolate
1½ tablespoons butter

❖ *P*reheat oven to 325 degrees. Grease bottom of 9x9 inch pan. Melt chocolate and butter in top of double boiler over hot water. Stir in sugar, eggs and peppermint extract. Stir in flour and salt. Spread in pan. Bake at 325 degrees for 25 minutes. Cool.

FILLING: Combine all filling ingredients. Spread over cooled brownies. Refrigerate.

GLAZE: Melt chocolate and butter in top of double boiler over hot water. Drizzle over cold filling, tilting pan until filling is entirely covered. Store in refrigerator.

ALMOND RASPBERRY TASSIES

Yield: 2 dozen

Pastry
- 1/2 cup butter, softened
- 1 (3-oz.) pkg. cream cheese, softened
- 1 cup all-purpose flour

Filling
- 1/4 cup raspberry preserves
- 1/2 cup sugar
- 1/2 cup almond paste
- 2 egg yolks
- 3 tablespoons all-purpose flour
- 2 tablespoons milk
- 1 tablespoon orange juice

❖ *P*ASTRY: Combine butter and cream cheese. Add flour. Cover and chill. Divide dough into 24 balls. Press into sides and bottom of mini muffin tins.

FILLING: Preheat oven to 400 degrees. Place 1/2 teaspoon raspberry preserves in bottom of each pastry shell. Combine sugar and almond paste. Add egg yolks one at a time, beating well after each addition. Stir in flour, milk and orange juice. Spoon into pastry shells. Bake at 400 degrees for 15 minutes. Cool; remove from pan. Store in refrigerator.

RUBY RED CRUNCH

Servings: 10

Filling
- 2 (10-oz.) pkgs. frozen raspberries, thawed and drained, reserving juice
- 1/2 cup sugar
- 3 teaspoons cornstarch
- 1 lb. sliced rhubarb, fresh or frozen

Crust
- 1 1/2 cups all-purpose flour, sifted
- 1 cup firmly packed brown sugar
- 1 cup quick-cooking oats
- 1 teaspoon cinnamon
- 1/2 cup butter or margarine melted

❖ *P*reheat oven to 350 degrees. Butter 9 x 9-inch pan.

FILLING: Add enough water to reserved raspberry juice to measure 1 cup. Combine juice, sugar and cornstarch in saucepan. Cook until thickened. Stir in raspberries and rhubarb.

CRUST: Combine all crust ingredients until crumbly. Press 2/3 of crust into prepared pan. Pour fruit mixture over crust. Top with remaining crumbs. Bake at 350 degrees for 1 hour. Serve warm or cold with whipped cream, vanilla ice cream or yogurt.

RASPBERRY BARS

Yield: 24 bars

1 cup butter, softened
1 cup sugar
2 egg yolks
1 teaspoon vanilla
2 cups all-purpose flour
1 (16-oz.) jar raspberry preserves
1 cup nuts, finely chopped
  Powdered sugar

❖ *P*reheat oven to 350 degrees. Grease 13 x 9-inch pan. Combine butter, sugar and egg yolks until well blended. Add vanilla and flour. Pat 1/2 of mixture into bottom of prepared pan. Spread preserves over dough. Sprinkle with nuts. Spread remaining dough over top of preserves. Bake at 350 degrees for 30 to 35 minutes. Cool and sprinkle with powdered sugar. Cut into squares.

CHOCOLATE TRUFFLE TART

Servings: 8-10

Crust
6 tablespoons butter, softened
1/2 cup sugar
3/4 cup all-purpose flour
1/3 cup cocoa
1/2 teaspoon vanilla
1/8 teaspoon salt
Filling
1 1/4 cups whipping cream
1 (12-oz.) pkg. semi-sweet chocolate chips
  White chocolate

❖ *C*RUST: Preheat oven to 350 degrees. Grease 10-inch springform or tart pan. Cream butter and sugar until light and fluffy. At low speed, beat in flour, cocoa, vanilla and salt until crumbly. Press dough into bottom and up sides of prepared pan. Bake at 350 degrees 8 to 10 minutes or until firm but not crisp. Cool completely on wire rack.

FILLING: Scald whipping cream. Remove from heat. Add chocolate; stir until melted and smooth. Cool until slightly thickened. Pour into prepared crust. Refrigerate tart 2 hours or until firm. Garnish with grated white chocolate or white chocolate curls.

CHOCOLATE APRICOT TORTE

Yield: 10-16 Servings

Filling

1	cup water
3/4	cup sugar
1	teaspoon lemon juice
1 1/2	teaspoons all-purpose flour
12	oz. dried apricots

Torte

2 1/3	cups semi-sweet chocolate chips
3/4	cup pecans
3/4	cup all-purpose flour
	Pinch of salt
2/3	cup firmly packed brown sugar
6	tablespoons butter, softened
1/2	teaspoon vanilla
1-3	tablespoons water
	Powdered sugar

❖ *FILLING:* In heavy saucepan, combine water, sugar, lemon juice and flour over high heat. Stir constantly until mixture comes to a boil. Reduce heat. Cook until mixture becomes very thick. Add apricots and simmer until mixture is a jam-like consistency. Set aside.

TORTE: Preheat oven to 350 degrees. Line the bottom of 2 (9 x 2-inch) round cake pans with parchment paper. Grease sides of pan. In large bowl, combine chocolate chips, pecans, flour, salt, brown sugar, butter and vanilla. Beat on low speed until well combined. Add water, a few drops at a time, just until batter reaches a "dough-like" consistency. Place 1/3 of chocolate mixture into each pan. Pat the mixture in the bottom and 2/3 up the sides of each pan. Divide filling evenly between prepared pans. Crumble the remaining chocolate mixture over the top of each torte. Bake at 350 degrees for 25 to 30 minutes or until filling bubbles and the sides are brown. Cool on wire racks. Dust with powdered sugar before serving.

This page has been underwritten through the generosity of CATHLEEN LANE.

CHOCOLATE BAUM KUCHEN

Servings: 10-12

Cake

- 1/3 **cup semi-sweet chocolate chips**
- 1/2 **cup butter, softened**
- 3/4 **cup sugar**
- 1 **teaspoon vanilla extract**
- 7 **egg yolks**
- 3 **tablespoons cornstarch**
- 2/3 **cup all-purpose flour**
- 7 **egg whites**

Garnish

- 2/3 **cup sour cream**
- 3 **tablespoons sugar**
- 1/2 **teaspoon lemon juice**

Chocolate Sour Cream Frosting

- 2/3 **cup semi-sweet chocolate chips**
- 3 **tablespoons butter**
- 1/2 **cup sour cream**
- 1/4 **teaspoon vanilla**
- 2-2½ **cups powdered sugar, sifted**
- 1½ **cups fresh strawberries, cleaned and hulled**

❖ CAKE: Adjust top oven rack 5 inches from broiler. Preheat broiler. Grease 9-inch springform pan. Melt chocolate chips in top of double boiler over hot water. Stir until smooth. Cool to room temperature. In small bowl, combine butter, 1/2 cup sugar and vanilla; beat until creamy. Add egg yolks, one at a time, beating well after each addition. Combine flour and cornstarch and add to butter mixture. Divide batter in half. Stir melted chocolate into 1/2 of batter. In large bowl, beat egg whites until soft peaks form. Gradually add 1/4 cup sugar, beating until stiff peaks form. Divide egg white evenly between plain and chocolate batter; fold gently. Batter may appear curdled. Spread scant 1/2 cup chocolate batter in bottom of prepared pan. Broil 30 to 45 seconds and check very frequently. Spread scant 1/2 cup plain batter on top of chocolate layer; broil. Repeat alternating chocolate and plain layers, building total of 10 layers.

GARNISH: Combine all garnish ingredients. Spread over top of cake. Broil 1 minute, or until set. Cool 10 to 15 minutes. Remove sides of pan; cool completely.

FROSTING: Combine chocolate and butter in top of double boiler over hot water. Stir until mixture is smooth. Transfer to small bowl. Stir in sour cream and vanilla. Gradually add powdered sugar, beating until frosting is smooth and spreading consistency. Frost sides of cooled cake with 2/3 of frosting. Arrange strawberries around edge of cake and center. Place remaining frosting in pastry bag. Pipe rosettes between rows of strawberries. Chill.

FLOURLESS GRAND MARNIER CAKE

with

RASPBERRY GINGER SAUCE

Servings: 10-12

Cake

1 1/2	cups sugar
7	tablespoons water
3	tablespoons Grand Marnier
8	oz. (8 squares) unsweetened chocolate, finely chopped
4	oz. semi-sweet chocolate, finely chopped
1	cup unsalted butter, softened
5	large eggs, room temperature
	Powdered sugar

Sauce

1	pint fresh raspberries
3	pieces candied ginger
1/4	cup Grenadine syrup
1/4	cup Framboise raspberry liqueur

❖ CAKE: Preheat oven to 350 degrees. Grease 9" x 1 1/2" round pan lined with wax paper. In heavy saucepan, combine 1 cup sugar, water and Grand Marnier; bring to a boil. Remove from heat. Add 4 oz. of unsweetened chocolate and 2 oz. of semi-sweet chocolate; stir until smooth. Whisk in remaining chocolate and butter until smooth; set aside. In large mixing bowl, beat eggs and 1/2 cup sugar until pale yellow and ribbons form when beaters are lifted. Beat in chocolate mixture until well blended. Pour batter into prepared pan. Place cake pan in a larger baking pan. Add enough boiling water in larger pan to fill 1/2 way up sides. Bake at 350 degrees for 30 minutes or until cake remains firm in center when shaken gently. Cake will still be slightly wet in center. Remove cake from water bath; cool 10 minutes. Unmold cake onto serving plate; cool completely. Sift powdered sugar over top of cake. Store loosely wrapped at room temperature.

SAUCE: In food processor, puree raspberries and ginger. Add Grenadine and Framboise and process until smooth. Pour and press through a strainer. Serve at room temperature.

To serve, spoon sauce onto plates and place cake wedges on top of sauce.

CHOCOLATE MOCHA RASPBERRY CAKE

Servings: 10-12

Cake

8	oz. (8 squares) semi-sweet chocolate
3	tablespoons instant coffee, powder or granules
1/4	cup Chambord, Creme de Cassis or berry liqueur
4	egg yolks
3/4	cup unsalted butter, divided
1/3	cup all-purpose flour
4	egg whites
1/3	cup sugar

Filling

1	pint fresh raspberries or 1 (8-oz.) pkg. frozen raspberries, thawed and drained
1/3	cup sugar
1/4	cup Chambord, cassis or berry liqueur

Glaze

4	oz. (4 squares) semi-sweet chocolate
5	tablespoons unsalted butter
1	tablespoon light corn syrup

❖ CAKE: Preheat oven to 375 degrees. Spray 9-inch springform pan with non-stick vegetable shortening spray. In heavy saucepan, combine chocolate, instant coffee and liqueur. Stir constantly over low heat until melted. Remove pan from heat. Add egg yolks one at a time, beating well after each addition. Return pan to heat. Cook, stirring constantly, for 2 minutes. Remove pan from heat and whisk in butter one tablespoon at a time. Stir in flour. Beat egg whites until soft peaks form; sprinkle with sugar and beat until glossy. Fold egg whites, in thirds, into chocolate mixture. Pour batter into prepared pan. Bake at 375 degrees for 20 minutes, or until cake is slightly puffy. Center will not be completely baked. Cool on wire rack for 45 minutes.

FILLING: Combine raspberries, sugar and liqueur in small bowl. Set aside.

GLAZE: In heavy saucepan over low heat, combine all glaze ingredients. Stir until smooth. Cool until mixture is tepid.

Unmold cake from pan. Scoop out top 1/2-inch of cake leaving a 1-inch border. Using a slotted spoon, place filling inside of cake. Spread glaze along the outside border of cake; make a criss-cross pattern with glaze across raspberries. Refrigerate for 30 minutes to set glaze. Serve chilled or at room temperature.

KIWI ICE

Servings: 8

1   cup sugar
1   cup water
9   ripe kiwis
¹/₄   cup freshly squeeze lime juice

❖ Combine sugar and water in 2-quart saucepan over medium-low heat; stir until sugar is dissolved. Increase heat and boil 5 minutes without stirring. Remove from heat; set aside. Cut 8 kiwis in half and remove pulp with teaspoon. Puree pulp in food processor or blender. Combine pulp, syrup and lime juice. Pour into a freezer container. Cover and freeze until mixture begins to harden, about 1 hour. Place mixture in bowl and beat until smooth and light. Freeze until firm. To serve, spoon into sherbet glasses. Peel remaining kiwi, slice and garnish each serving.

WHITE CHOCOLATE ICE CREAM

Yield: 2 quarts

2   cups half-and-half
12   oz. premium quality white chocolate
4   eggs
2   cups whipping cream
1¹/₂   cups sugar

❖ Place half-and-half in top of double boiler over boiling water; scald. Reduce heat. Add chocolate; cook until smooth and melted. Remove from heat. Combine eggs and whipping cream in large bowl. Add sugar and beat until dissolved. Slowly stir in chocolate mixture. Refrigerate until well chilled. Process mixture in ice cream maker following manufacturer's instructions. Freeze in covered container for 4 hours.

FROZEN
RASPBERRY MOUSSE
with
MELBA SAUCE

Servings: 8

Mousse

- 1 **(10-oz.) pkg. frozen raspberries in syrup**
- 1 **cup whipping cream, whipped**
- 1 **(8-oz.) carton raspberry yogurt**
- 1 **egg white**
- 1/4 **cup sugar**

Melba Sauce

- 1 **(10-oz.) pkg. frozen raspberries in syrup, thawed**
- 1 **(12-oz.) pkg. frozen sliced peaches in syrup, thawed**
- 1 **tablespoon cornstarch**
- 1 **tablespoon water**
- 2 **tablespoons Kirsch**

❖ MOUSSE: Place frozen raspberries in food processor or blender. Process until smooth. Add raspberry puree to whipped cream; fold in yogurt. Beat egg white, gradually adding sugar until soft peaks form. Fold egg whites into raspberry mixture. Spoon into 4-cup mold or decorative bowl; cover with plastic wrap. Freeze until firm. Remove from freezer and place in refrigerator 30 minutes before serving. Just before serving, dip mold quickly in warm water, run sharp knife around edge and invert onto serving platter. Drizzle with Melba Sauce.

MELBA SAUCE: Puree raspberries and peaches. In medium saucepan, dissolve cornstarch in water. Add fruit puree. Cook over medium heat, stirring constantly, until sauce is thick and clear; strain. Stir in Kirsch. Chill thoroughly.

COFFEE CARAMEL
PARFAITS

Servings: 8

Sauce

- 3/4 **cup sugar**
- 1/4 **cup water**
- 1/4 **cup light corn syrup**
- 1/2 **cup whipping cream**
- 5 **tablespoons unsalted butter**
- 1/3 **cup sour cream**

Parfait

- 1/3 **cup sugar**
- 1/4 **cup whipping cream**
- 6 **egg yolks**
- 2 **tablespoons instant coffee powder or granules**
- 2 **oz. imported white chocolate, chopped**
- 2 **tablespoons Kahlua**
- 3/4 **cup whipping cream**
- 1/2 **cup sour cream**
- 1 **cup toasted pecans**

Topping

- 1/2 **cup whipping cream**
- 1 **teaspoon powdered sugar**
- 1/2 **teaspoon vanilla**

❖ *S*AUCE: Combine sugar, water and corn syrup in heavy medium saucepan. Cook over low heat until sugar is dissolved. Increase heat and boil without stirring until mixture becomes a deep golden brown. Add whipping cream and butter; whisk until smooth. Remove from heat and whisk in sour cream. Spoon 1 tablespoon sauce into parfait glasses.

PARFAIT: In top of double boiler, combine sugar, cream, egg yolks and coffee powder over boiling water; whisk for 3 minutes. Remove from heat. Whisk in white chocolate and Kahlua until smooth. Beat mixture on high speed until cool and thick, about 5 minutes. Combine 3/4 cup whipping cream and sour cream and beat until soft peaks form. Fold in coffee mixture. Spoon 1/3 cup mixture into each parfait glass; freeze 1 hour. Refrigerate remaining parfait mixture. Spoon 2 tablespoons sauce into each glass, tilting glass slightly to completely cover parfait. Sprinkle each with 2 tablespoons chopped pecans. Freeze 20 minutes. Divide remaining parfait mixture between glasses; freeze 1 hour. Drizzle 1 tablespoon sauce over each.

TOPPING: Whip cream, sugar and vanilla until soft peaks form. To serve, place dollop of whipped cream on each parfait.

CHOCOLATE
MOUSSE CAKE

Servings: 10-12

Crust

12 oz. finely crushed chocolate wafer crumbs

10 tablespoons unsalted butter, melted

Filling

16 oz. (16 squares) semi-sweet chocolate

2 eggs

4 egg yolks

2 cups whipping cream

6 tablespoons powdered sugar

6 egg whites, room temperature

Garnish

2 cups whipping cream

Sugar

❖ CRUST: Combine crust ingredients. Press on bottom and completely up sides of 9-inch springform pan. Refrigerate for 30 minutes or chill in freezer.

FILLING: Melt chocolate in top of double boiler over hot water; cool to lukewarm. Add whole eggs and mix well. Add egg yolks and mix until blended. Whip cream with powdered sugar until soft peaks form. Beat egg white until stiff but not dry.

Fold whipped cream into chocolate mixture. Fold in egg whites until completely incorporated. Pour into crust and refrigerate 6 hours or overnight.

GARNISH: Whip cream with sugar to taste until stiff.

Run sharp knife around crust to loosen; remove ring. Reserve 1/2 cup whipped cream. Spread remaining whipped cream over top of mousse. Pipe reserved whipped cream rosettes in center of cake.

This page has been underwritten through the generosity of BONNIE FEMEC.

CHOCOLATE VELVET CHEESECAKE

Crust

   2   tablespoons unsalted butter, softened

   1   (8½-oz.) pkg. chocolate wafer cookies, finely ground

       Pinch salt

  ⅛   teaspoon cinnamon

  ⅓   cup unsalted butter, melted and cooled

Filling

  12   oz. (12 squares) semi-sweet chocolate

   2   tablespoons unsalted butter

   3   (8-oz.) pkgs. cream cheese, cubed and softened

  1½   cups whipping cream

   1   teaspoon vanilla

   1   cup sugar

   3   large eggs, at room temperature, slightly beaten

   2   tablespoons unsweetened cocoa powder

       Powdered sugar

❖ CRUST: Preheat oven to 350 degrees. Butter 9-inch springform pan with 2 tablespoons butter. Combine cookie crumbs, salt and cinnamon in medium bowl. Drizzle melted butter over mixture; stir with fork until well blended. Press in bottom of prepared pan.

FILLING: Combine chocolate with butter in top of double boiler over hot water until chocolate is completely melted. Remove from heat. Stir until smooth. Reserve at room temperature, uncovered. Beat cream cheese in large bowl until completely smooth. Gradually beat in chocolate mixture. Continue beating, scraping down sides, until mixture is smooth and uniform in color. Gradually add cream and vanilla; beat until well blended. Gradually add sugar, beating constantly until sugar is absorbed. Add eggs, ¼ at a time, beating well after each addition. Sift cocoa over batter. Beat at low speed until cocoa is thoroughly incorporated. Pour batter into prepared pan; smooth top. Gently rotate pan several quarter turns to settle batter. Bake at 350 degrees for 30 minutes. Reduce oven temperature to 325 degrees; continue baking 30 minutes longer. Turn off oven. Let cake stand in oven with door ajar 30 minutes. Transfer pan to wire rack away from drafts. Let cool undisturbed until sides and bottom are room temperature. Remove springform; cover loosely with foil. Refrigerate 8 hours or overnight. To serve, sift powdered sugar over top.

CHEESECAKE PUMPKIN PIE

Servings: 8

  1   (9-inch) unbaked pie shell
Cheese Cake Layer
  1   (8-oz.) pkg. cream cheese, softened
  1/4   cup sugar
  1/4   teaspoon vanilla
  1   egg
Pumpkin Layer
  1 1/4   cups canned pumpkin
  1/2   cup sugar
  1/4   cup evaporated milk
  2   eggs, beaten
  1   teaspoon cinnamon
  1/4   teaspoon ground ginger
  1/4   teaspoon nutmeg
        Dash salt
Garnish
  2   tablespoons maple syrup
  24   pecan halves

❖ CHEESE CAKE LAYER: Preheat oven to 350 degrees. Beat cream cheese, sugar and vanilla until well blended. Add egg; beat until well combined. Spread in bottom of pie shell.

PUMPKIN LAYER: Combine pumpkin, sugar, milk, eggs, cinnamon, ginger, nutmeg and salt until well blended. Carefully pour over cheese cake layer. Bake at 350 degrees for 65 minutes. Cool. Brush with syrup; garnish with pecan halves. Store in refrigerator.

FROZEN MOCHA CHEESECAKE

Servings: 8-10

Crust
  1 1/4   cups finely crushed chocolate wafer crumbs (about 24 wafers)
  1/4   cup sugar
  1/4   cup butter or margarine, melted
Filling
  1   (8-oz.) pkg. cream cheese, softened
  1   (14-oz.) can sweetened condensed milk
  2/3   cup chocolate syrup
  2   tablespoons instant coffee powder or granules
  1   teaspoon hot water
  1   cup whipping cream, whipped

❖ CRUST: Combine crumbs, sugar and butter; press in bottom of 9-inch springform pan.

FILLING: In large bowl, beat cream cheese until fluffy. Add milk and chocolate syrup. In small bowl, dissolve coffee in water. Add to cream cheese mixture; blend well. Fold in whipped cream. Pour into crust. Cover and freeze for 6 hours or until firm. Remove from freezer and refrigerate 30 minutes before serving. Cut into wedges; garnish with dollop of whipped cream and shaved chocolate.

KEY LIME
CHEESECAKE

Servings: 10-12

Crust

- 1¼ **cups gingersnap crumbs**
- 2 **tablespoons sugar**
- 5 **tablespoons unsalted butter, melted**

Filling

- 3 **(8-oz.) pkg. cream cheese, softened**
- 1½ **cups sugar**
- 4 **large eggs**
- ¼ **cup fresh lime juice**
- 2 **tablespoons grated lime peel**

Topping

- 1 **pint sour cream**
- ⅓ **cup sugar**
- 2 **tablespoons fresh lime juice**
- 2 **tablespoons grated lime peel**

  Halved lime slices or julienned lime peel

❖ CRUST: Preheat oven to 350 degrees. In small bowl, combine all crust ingredients with fork. Press firmly on bottom and halfway up sides of 9-inch springform pan.

FILLING: Beat cream cheese with sugar until smooth. On lowest speed, beat in eggs, one at a time. Blend in lime juice and lime peel. Pour into prepared pan. Bake at 350 degrees for 40 minutes or until edges are light brown and pulling away slightly from side of pan. Center will not be completely set.

TOPPING: While cake is baking, whisk together sour cream, sugar, lime juice and lime peel. When cake is done, spoon topping over cake, beginning at edge of pan. Smooth gently. Return to oven and bake 10 minutes. Cool cake to room temperature on wire rack; refrigerate 4 hours or overnight until very cold. To serve, garnish with lime slices or peel.

TORTA MASCARPONE

Serves: 10-12

1 cup Mascarpone cheese

1/2 cup powdered sugar, sifted

1/3 cup Marsala wine

1 teaspoon vanilla

3 oz. (3 squares) premium semi-sweet chocolate, grated

2 egg whites

1 cup whipping cream, whipped

20 Amaretti cookies (Italian almond macaroons), crushed

12 large strawberries, sliced in half

❖ *I*n large bowl, beat cheese until smooth. Stir in sugar, wine and vanilla. Fold in grated chocolate. Using clean, dry beaters, beat egg whites until stiff but not dry. Gently fold whipped cream into Mascarpone mixture; fold in egg whites just until incorporated. Spoon 1/2 of mixture into 9-inch springform pan. Sprinkle 3/4 of crushed Amaretti over top. Cover with remaining Mascarpone mixture; sprinkle top with remaining Amaretti. Cover with plastic wrap and freeze 2-3 hours. Place torta in refrigerator until served. To serve, unmold, slice and garnish with sliced strawberries.

VARIATION: White Chocolate Torta – substitute white chocolate for semi-sweet, 1/4 cup Amaretto for Marsala wine and reduce powdered sugar to 1/3 cup.

BEST EVER CHEESECAKE

Servings: 8-12

Crust

2 cups graham cracker crumbs

1/3 cup sugar

1/2 cup unsalted butter, softened

Filling

2 (8-oz.) pkg. cream cheese

1 cup sugar

3 large eggs

3 tablespoons fresh lemon juice

1 1/2 teaspoons vanilla

1/4 teaspoons salt

3 cups sour cream

❖ *C*RUST: Preheat oven to 350 degrees. Grease 8 x 2 1/2-inch springform pan. Combine graham cracker crumbs, sugar and butter. Press on bottom and up sides of prepared pan.

FILLING: In large mixing bowl, beat cream cheese with sugar for 3 minutes or until very smooth. Add eggs, one at a time, beating well after each addition. Add lemon juice, vanilla and salt and beat until well blended. Add sour cream; beat just until blended. Pour batter into prepared pan. Set the pan in a larger pan and fill with hot water to a depth of one inch. Bake at 350 degrees for 45 minutes. Turn off oven without opening door and allow to stand in oven for 1 hour. Remove to a rack and allow to cool for 1 hour. Cover with plastic wrap and refrigerate overnight. To unmold, wipe sides of pan with hot, damp cloth. Run a knife around edge of pan; release ring mold.

THREE LAYER
CARROT CAKE

Servings: 12

Cake

1¼	cups vegetable oil
1¾	cups sugar
2	cups all-purpose flour
2	teaspoons baking soda
1	teaspoon salt
4	eggs
1	lb. carrots, grated
1	cup chopped pecans or walnuts
1	cup raisins

Filling

¾	cup sugar
¼	cup flour
1	cup whipping cream
¼	cup butter or margarine
¼	teaspoon salt
1	cup chopped pecans or walnuts
2	teaspoons vanilla

Frosting

4	oz. shredded coconut
1	(8-oz.) pkg. cream cheese, softened
1	cup butter or margarine, softened
3	cups powdered sugar
1	teaspoon vanilla

❖ CAKE: Grease 10-inch tube pan. In large bowl, beat oil and sugar for 2 to 3 minutes. Combine flour, baking soda and salt. Sift ½ of flour into sugar mixture; blend well. Sift in remaining flour, alternating with eggs, mixing well after each addition. Stir in carrots, nuts and raisins. Pour batter into prepared pan. Bake at 325 degrees for 1 hour and 10 minutes. Cool in pan.

FILLING: Blend sugar and flour in small saucepan. Slowly stir in cream. Add butter and salt. Cook over low heat, stirring until mixture comes to a simmer, about 30 minutes. Simmer 2 to 3 minutes. Remove from heat and cool to lukewarm. Stir in nuts and vanilla. Cool completely.

FROSTING: Preheat oven to 300 degrees. Spread coconut on baking sheet. Bake for 10 to 15 minutes, or until coconut is toasted. Cool. Blend cream cheese and butter. Add sugar and vanilla; beat until smooth. Refrigerate for 30 minutes. Slice cooled cake into 3 layers. Spread filling between each layer. Reassemble on cake plate and frost. Garnish cake with toasted coconut.

BLUEBERRIES
and PEACHES in
MINT SAUCE

Servings: 4

4   peaches, peeled, pitted and sliced

1/3 pint blueberries, rinsed

3   tablespoons fresh lemon juice

1/4 cup loosely packed fresh mint, chopped

4   teaspoons sugar

❖ Combine peaches and blueberries in bowl. In blender or food processor, blend lemon juice, mint and sugar. Pour over fruit and toss lightly. Chill before serving.

FRESH PEACH
SOUR CREAM PIE

Servings: 8

1   (9-inch) unbaked pie shell

5-6 medium fresh peaches, peeled, pitted and halved

1   cup sour cream

1/2 cup sugar

1/3 cup firmly packed brown sugar

1   cup all-purpose flour

❖ Place peaches in pie shell. Combine sour cream, sugar, brown sugar and flour. Spoon over peaches. Bake at 450 degrees for 10 minutes. Reduce oven temperature to 325 degrees and continue baking for 25 to 30 minutes or until top is browned.

APPLE-NUT TORTE

Servings: 6

- 1/2 cup plus 2 tablespoons sugar
- 1/2 cup all-purpose flour
- 2 teaspoons baking powder
- 1/4 teaspoon cinnamon
- 1 egg, beaten
- 1 cup chopped apples
- 1 cup chopped walnuts
- 1 teaspoon vanilla

❖ *P*reheat oven to 375 degrees. Lightly grease 9-inch springform pan. In large bowl, combine sugar, flour, baking powder and cinnamon. In small bowl, combine egg, apples, walnuts and vanilla; mix well. Stir apple mixture into dry mixture. Spread into prepared pan. Bake at 375 degrees for 30 to 45 minutes. Serve with sweetened whipped cream or vanilla ice cream.

SOUR CHERRY GÂTEAU

Servings: 6

Gateau
- 1 (16-oz.) can sour cherries, drained, reserve juice
- 1/4 cup sugar
- 1 cup all-purpose flour
- 1 teaspoon baking soda
- 1 teaspoon cinnamon
- 1 egg, beaten
- 1 tablespoon butter, melted
- 1/2 cup chopped walnuts

Sauce
- 1/2 cup sugar
- 1 teaspoon butter
- 1 tablespoon cornstarch
- Reserved cherry juice

❖ *P*reheat oven to 350 degrees. Grease 8 x 8-inch pan. Combine sugar, flour, soda and cinnamon. Stir in egg, butter, cherries and walnuts. Pour into prepared pan. Bake at 350 degrees for 35 to 45 minutes. Cool completely on rack. Serve with sauce and dollop of whipped cream, if desired.

SAUCE: In saucepan, over medium heat, combine sugar, butter, cornstarch and reserved cherry juice, stirring constantly until mixture is thick and clear; cool.

APPLESAUCE RAISIN CAKE with CARAMEL ICING

Servings: 10-12

Cake

2¹/₂	cups raisins
1	cup butter, softened
2	cups sugar
3	eggs
2¹/₂	cups unsweetened applesauce
4	cups all-purpose flour
4	teaspoons baking soda
1	teaspoon ground cloves
1	teaspoon cinnamon
³/₄	teaspoon salt
1	cup chopped walnuts

Icing

¹/₂	cup butter, softened
1	cup firmly packed brown sugar
¹/₄	cup whipping cream
3¹/₂	cups (1 lb.) powdered sugar

❖ CAKE: Preheat oven to 325 degrees. Grease and flour 10-inch tube pan. Place raisins in small bowl. Pour boiling water over raisins. Allow to set 10 minutes. In large bowl, cream butter and sugar until light and fluffy. Add eggs, one at a time, beating well after each addition. Stir in applesauce. Sift flour, baking soda, cloves, cinnamon and salt; add to batter. Drain raisins well. Dust with 1 to 2 tablespoons flour. Stir raisins and nuts into batter. Pour into prepared pan. Bake at 325 degrees for 1 ¹/₂ hours. Cool completely.

ICING: Melt butter in large saucepan. Add brown sugar. Slowly bring to a boil. Stir for 1 minute or until slightly thick. Add cream, stirring over low heat until smooth. Remove from heat and cool slightly. Beat in powdered sugar until spreading consistency. Cool. Frost cooled cake.

The Old Arcade

FRESH FRUIT TRIFLE

Servings: 10-12

2 cups milk

4 egg yolks

1/2 cup sugar

3 tablespoons cornstarch

1/4 teaspoon salt

2 tablespoons butter

1 teaspoon vanilla

2 (12-oz.) pkgs. pound cake, cut into 1/2-inch slices

1/2 cup Grand Marnier

1 lb. strawberries, cleaned, hulled and sliced

2 bananas, sliced

1 (11-oz.) can mandarin oranges, drained

2 kiwis, peeled and sliced

1 pint fresh blueberries

1 cup whipping cream

2 tablespoons powdered sugar

Whole strawberries

❖ Combine milk, egg yolks, sugar, cornstarch and salt in food processor or blender. Process until well blended. Pour into medium size glass bowl. Microwave on high for 6 to 7 minutes or until thickened. Stir halfway through cooking. (Custard can also be prepared in saucepan. Cook over medium heat, stirring constantly, until thickened.) Whisk in butter and vanilla. Cover and refrigerate until cool and soft set. Brush cake slices with Grand Marnier. Arrange half the slices in a single layer in trifle or deep glass bowl. Layer 1/2 of strawberries, bananas, oranges, kiwis and blueberries. Spoon 1/2 of custard mixture over fruit. Repeat. Whip cream until soft peaks form. Add powdered sugar and continue beating until stiff. Spoon or pipe decoratively over top of trifle. Garnish with whole strawberries. Chill until ready to serve.

STRAWBERRY MERINGUE TORTE

Servings: 10

Meringue

4	**egg whites, room temperature**
1/2	**teaspoon cream of tartar**
1/4	**teaspoon salt**
2	**cups powdered sugar**

Filling

1	**(12-oz.) pkg. semi-sweet chocolate chips**
6	**tablespoons water**
3	**cups whipping cream**
1/3	**cup sugar**
2	**pints fresh strawberries, cleaned and sliced**
1	**pint fresh strawberries, cleaned and halved**

❖ MERINGUE: Preheat oven to 250 degrees. Beat egg whites with cream of tartar and salt until soft peaks form. Slowly add sugar, 1 tablespoon at a time, beating until mixture is stiff, about 20 minutes. Draw 3 (9-inch) circles on parchment paper; place on cookie sheet. Spread 1/3 of meringue mixture on each circle. Bake at 250 degrees for 1 hour. Turn oven off and allow meringues to cool in oven.

FILLING: Melt chocolate with water in saucepan; set aside. Whip cream until soft peaks form. Gradually add sugar and beat until stiff. Place a meringue shell on serving plate. Spread with thin layer of chocolate. Top with 1/3 whipped cream and 1/2 of sliced strawberries. Repeat. Top with last meringue shell and frost with remaining whipped cream. Drizzle remaining chocolate over top. Decorate with halved strawberries. Refrigerate 3 hours before serving.

Health

The Cleveland Clinic reflecting East Mount Zion Church

This chapter of permissible pleasures offers many healthy surprises. Together with the renowned Cleveland Clinic Foundation, we have compiled recipes that are both easy and good for you. Here we offer you flavorful treats that are truly inspired by good health and good taste.

This section has been underwritten through the generosity of
THE CLEVELAND CLINIC FOUNDATION.

CREAMY RED PEPPER CROUTONS

Servings: 6

Red Pepper Spread

- 1/2 teaspoon chopped garlic
- 1 (5-oz.) jar red peppers, drained
- 2 tablespoons 1% lowfat cottage cheese
- 2 oz. (1/4 cup) Neufchatel or lite cream cheese, softened
- 1 teaspoon fresh dill
- 1/8 teaspoon fresh ground black pepper
- 2 teaspoons lemon juice

- 1 (6-oz.) baguette French bread
- Fresh dill sprigs

❖ RED PEPPER SPREAD: Preheat oven to 400 degrees. Place garlic, red peppers, cottage cheese, cream cheese, dill, black pepper and lemon juice in food processor. Process until smooth.

Cut bread into 42 to 48 thin slices. Arrange bread slices on cookie sheet. Bake at 400 degrees for 10 minutes or until crisp. Spread croutons with Red Pepper Spread. Garnish with small sprig of fresh dill.

Fat: 3.5 grams
Cholesterol: 8 milligrams
Sodium: 296 milligrams
Calories: 129 per serving

EGGPLANT ORIENTAL on TOMATO ROUNDS

Servings: 6

- 2 (1-lb.) eggplants
- 3-5 cloves garlic, chopped
- 3 1/2 tablespoons chopped fresh ginger
- 2 tablespoons soy sauce
- 1 tablespoon dark sesame oil
- 3 tablespoons fresh chopped cilantro
- 1/4 teaspoon hot chile oil or Tabasco sauce
- 1 tablespoon rice wine vinegar
- 1/2 teaspoon sugar
- 12 tomato slices

❖ Preheat oven to 400 degrees. Place eggplants on cookie sheet and bake at 400 degrees for 1 hour. When cool enough to handle, peel and cut into 1/2-inch cubes.

In large bowl, combine garlic, ginger, soy sauce, sesame oil, cilantro, chile oil, vinegar and sugar. Stir in 3 1/2 cups eggplant. Arrange 2 tomato slices on each of 6 individual serving plates. Spoon eggplant mixture evenly over tomato slices. Serve.

Fat: 2.8 grams
Cholesterol: 0
Sodium: 355 milligrams
Calories: 84 per serving

COLD PEACH SOUP

Servings: 8

1½   cups cold water

4   cloves

¾   cup sugar

1   cinnamon stick, broken into small pieces

2   tablespoons cornstarch

¼   cup cold water

1½   cups dry white wine

3½   lbs. (about 12) ripe peaches, peeled and pitted

1   cup fresh blueberries

❖ *P*lace 1 ½ cups cold water, cloves, sugar and cinnamon in small saucepan; bring to a boil. Simmer 10 minutes. Dissolve cornstarch in ¼ cup water; whisk into sugar mixture. Bring to a boil; set aside to cool. When cool, remove cinnamon sticks and cloves. Stir wine into syrup; refrigerate. Slice 2 cups of peaches for garnish. Puree remaining peaches in food processor or blender. Combine syrup, peach puree and peach slices. Refrigerate several hours or overnight. To serve, fill individual bowls with soup and garnish with blueberries.

Fat: 0.3 grams
Cholesterol: 0
Sodium: 7 milligrams
Calories: 207 per serving

CARROT and GINGER SOUP

Servings: 6

1   tablespoon canola oil

2   large onions

¼   cup chopped fresh ginger

4   cloves garlic, minced

7   cups chicken or light vegetable stock

1   cup dry white wine

2   lbs. carrots, peeled and sliced

3   tablespoons lemon juice

2   teaspoons curry powder

   Salt and pepper to taste

❖ *S*aute onions and ginger in oil. Add garlic. Stir in chicken stock, wine and carrots. Bring to a boil. Add lemon juice, curry powder, salt and pepper. Simmer for 45 minutes or until carrots are tender. Puree in food processor or blender. Serve warm or cold. Garnish with dash of nutmeg or dollop of sour cream or lowfat yogurt.

Fat: 1.5 grams
Cholesterol: 0
Sodium: 217 milligrams
Calories: 70 per serving

BLUEBERRY MUFFINS

Yield: 30 muffins

1   cup all-purpose flour
2   cups whole wheat flour
2   teaspoons baking soda
1   teaspoon salt
1   cup firmly packed brown sugar
2   tablespoons melted margarine
     or vegetable oil
1¹/₂ cups lowfat buttermilk
2   egg whites
³/₄ cup blueberries

❖ Combine flour, soda, salt and brown sugar. Stir in margarine, buttermilk and egg whites; beat until smooth. Gently fold blueberries into batter. Allow to stand 20 minutes. Preheat oven to 350 degrees. Line muffin cups with paper baking cups. Spoon batter into prepared muffin pan. Bake at 350 degrees for 20 to 25 minutes.

Fat: 1 gram
Cholesterol: < 1 milligram
Sodium: 118 milligrams
Calories: 85 per muffin

BRAISED ENDIVE

Servings: 6

6   (2¹/₂ to 3 oz.) heads Belgian endive,
     cleaned and trimmed
1   teaspoon sugar
¹/₂ teaspoon salt
1¹/₂ teaspoons safflower or canola oil
¹/₂ cup water

❖ If endive is very large, cut in half lengthwise. Arrange in single layer in stainless steel saucepan. Sprinkle with sugar, salt and oil. Pour water over endive. Place inverted plate over endive. Bring to a boil. Lower heat and simmer, covered, 20 minutes. Remove cover and plate; boil over high heat until liquid is reduced to 2 to 3 tablespoons. Arrange in star pattern on plate. Pour cooking juices over endive and serve.

Fat: 1/3 grams
Cholesterol: 0
Sodium: 180 milligrams
Calories: 24 per serving

HERBED
ONION PIZZA

Servings: 4

Dough

1	**pkg. active dry yeast**
1¼	**cups warm water (105 degrees to 115 degrees)**
1	**tablespoon sugar**
2	**cups all-purpose flour**
1	**teaspoon dried basil**
1	**teaspoon dried sage**
1	**teaspoon dried parsley**

Topping

6	**tablespoons honey or spicy mustard**
6	**onions, thinly sliced**
6	**cloves garlic, unpeeled**

❖ *D*OUGH: Dissolve yeast in warm water with sugar. Allow to set 10 minutes or until yeast is foamy. In food processor, combine flour, basil, sage and parsley. With machine running, add dissolved yeast. Process until dough forms a ball. Place in bowl; cover and let rise for 1 hour or until doubled in size. Spray cookie sheet with non-stick vegetable spray. Sprinkle lightly with cornmeal. Separate dough into 2 balls. Roll each to a thickness of ¼-inch. Place on prepared cookie sheet.

TOPPING: While dough is rising, roast garlic cloves in skins at 325 degrees for 30 to 45 minutes or until tender. Remove skins and chop. Spray skillet with non-stick vegetable spray. Saute onions until soft golden brown. Preheat oven to 375 degrees. Spread 3 tablespoons mustard on each pizza round. Arrange half of onion slices and chopped garlic on each. Bake at 375 degrees for 20 minutes.

Fat: 0.7 grams
Cholesterol: 0
Sodium: 78 milligrams
Calories: 110 per slice

A country herb garden in Gates Mills

CREAMY CUCUMBER DRESSING

Yield: 2 cups
(Sixteen 2-tablespoon servings)

3/4   cup cucumber peeled, seeded and coarsely chopped

2   tablespoons dill

1   teaspoon jalapeno pepper, seeded

3   cloves garlic

2   tablespoons lemon juice

1 1/2   cups plain non-fat yogurt

2   tablespoons olive oil

1/2   teaspoon salt

2   teaspoons sugar

❖ *P*lace garlic in food processor. Process until finely minced. Add cucumber, dill and jalapeno pepper. Process until smooth. Combine with remaining ingredients. Chill.

Fat: 1.8 grams
Cholesterol: 0
Sodium: 78 milligrams
Calories: 31 per serving

CHICKEN in LIME and YOGURT SAUCE

Servings: 6

6   (6-oz.) chicken breasts, skinned, boned and trimmed of all fat

Marinade

2   green onions, chopped

4   cloves garlic

1   teaspoon ground cumin

1/2   teaspoon caraway seeds

1/2   teaspoon freshly ground black pepper

1/2   teaspoon salt

2   teaspoon coriander seed, crushed

6   strips lime peel, coarsely chopped

2   tablespoons lime juice

2/3   cup plain non-fat yogurt

❖ *M*ARINADE: Combine all marinade ingredients. Roll chicken pieces in marinade and arrange in a stainless steel pan that will fit under broiler. Cover with plastic wrap. Allow to stand 1 hour at room temperature or refrigerated overnight. Preheat broiler. Pour off all but 1/4 cup of marinade. Broil chicken 8-inches from heat for 5 minutes on each side. Slice chicken on diagonal and serve.

Fat: 6.4 grams
Cholesterol: 146 milligrams
Sodium: 310 milligrams
Calories: 306 per serving

VEGETARIAN
MANICOTTI

Servings: 10

Sauce

2	medium onions, chopped
2	large green peppers, finely chopped
4	cloves garlic, minced
1/2	cup chopped fresh parsley
1	teaspoon dried oregano
2	teaspoons dried basil
2	(16-oz.) cans tomatoes
2	(6-oz.) cans tomato paste
4	cups water
2	bay leaves
1/4	cup sugar
1/2	teaspoon black pepper
1/2	cup dry red wine
12	oz. fresh tofu, mashed
2 1/2	cups 1% lowfat cottage cheese
1	medium onion, finely chopped
3	tablespoons fresh chopped parsley
3	egg whites
1/4	cup plain bread crumbs
20	manicotti shells, uncooked

❖ *S*AUCE: In a large non-stick skillet, combine all sauce ingredients. Cover tightly and simmer for 2 hours, stirring occasionally.

Preheat oven to 350 degrees. In large bowl, combine tofu, cottage cheese, onion, parsley, egg whites and bread crumbs. Stuff mixture into uncooked shells. Pour 1 cup of sauce in each of two 11 x 7-inch pans. Place stuffed manicotti in single layer in prepared pans. Cover with remaining sauce. Cover with foil and bake at 350 degrees for 50 to 60 minutes or until manicotti shells are tender.

NOTE: Sauce is also excellent served over spaghetti.

Fat: 3 grams
Cholesterol: 2 milligrams
Calories: 192 per serving

Celebrations

The Cleveland Museum of Art celebrates its 75th birthday

Who needs a formal celebration to enjoy sensational food? Good food truly is the mark of a special occasion—an intimate dinner for two, afternoon tea in the garden, a picnic in the country, a small gathering of friends wherever and whenever you please. You needn't wait for an extravagant occasion. Treasure the moment and let your spirit of celebration soar.

This section has been underwritten through the generosity of CLEVELAND MENU PRINTING.

RUBY PUNCH

Yield: 20 servings

1 (12-oz.) can frozen lemonade, prepared as directed
1 quart cranberry juice cocktail, chilled
1 (32-oz.) bottle ginger ale, chilled
1 (6-oz.) can frozen orange juice concentrate, thawed
  Orange slices

❖ Combine lemonade, cranberry juice, ginger ale and orange juice in punch bowl; stir to mix. Float orange slices in punch.

HOT HOLIDAY PUNCH

Yield: 40 servings

3 quarts apple juice
1 (48-oz.) bottle cranberry juice cocktail
1/2 cup firmly packed brown sugar
4 cinnamon sticks
11/2 teaspoons whole cloves
1/2 teaspoon salt

❖ Combine all ingredients in large saucepan. Bring to a simmer; stirring until sugar is dissolved. Serve hot.

SGROPIN

Yield: 2 servings

1 tablespoon freshly squeezed lemon juice
1-2 oz. vodka
2 scoops premium quality vanilla ice cream
2 ice cubes

❖ Place all ingredients in blender; whip until smooth.

CITRUS COOLER

Yield: 34 servings

1 (6-oz.) can frozen lemonade concentrate, thawed
1 (6-oz.) can frozen orange juice concentrate, thawed
1 (6-oz.) can frozen pineapple juice concentrate, thawed
21/2 cups cold water
1 (2 liter) bottle ginger ale, chilled

❖ Combine lemonade, orange juice, pineapple juice and water in punch bowl. Add ginger ale and mix well.

CHOCOLATE MINT SMOOTHIE

Servings: 4

¹/₄   cup white creme de menthe
¹/₄   cup creme de cocoa
 1   quart chocolate ice cream
      Mint sprigs
      Chocolate curls
      Peppermint candy

❖ *P*our creme de menthe and creme de cocoa into blender. Add ice cream, a spoonful at a time, blending smooth after each addition. Pour into glasses and serve immediately. Garnish with mint, chocolate curls or peppermint.

HUNTER'S COCKTAIL

Yield: 4 servings

 4   oz. bourbon
 4   oz. brandy
 1   oz. maple syrup
 1   dash Angostura bitters
 1   oz. Grenadine syrup

❖ *C*ombine all ingredients; stir well. Serve in small cocktail glasses over ice.

MARTY'S OLD-FASHIONED

Yield: 1 serving

1¹/₄   oz. Jack Daniels Tennessee Whiskey
 1   oz. maraschino cherry juice
 1   tablespoon sugar
 3   dashes Angostura bitters
 3   oz. club soda
 2   maraschino cherries
      Orange slice
      Ice cubes

❖ *F*ill one 10-oz. glass with ice; pour whiskey over ice. In another 10-oz. glass, combine cherry juice, sugar and bitters, stirring well for 10-15 seconds. Add club soda. Pour mixture over Jack Daniels and ice. Garnish with orange slice and cherries.

SCARLETT O'HARA PUNCH

Yield: 8 servings

 1   cup cranberry juice cocktail
 1   cup Southern Comfort
 3   cups lemon-lime soda
 3   oz. lemon juice

❖ *C*ombine all ingredients and serve chilled with ice.

CHILDREN'S PARTY

Peachy Keen Party Punch
Pizza Burgers
Hot, Hot Beans
Crunchy Fudge Bars

PEACHY KEEN PARTY PUNCH

Servings: 12-15

4	cups ice
1$^{1}/_{2}$	cups white grape juice
1	(20-oz.) can peach halves in syrup
$^{1}/_{2}$	gallon peach ice cream
2	cups ginger ale

❖ *P*lace ice in punch bowl. In two batches, combine grape juice and peach halves with syrup and ice cream in food processor or blender. Process for 20 to 30 seconds. Pour into punch bowl. Slowly add ginger ale to mixture.

PIZZA BURGERS

Servings: 6

1	lb. ground beef
1	cup prepared pizza sauce
$^{1}/_{8}$	teaspoon onion salt
1	clove garlic, minced
	Salt and pepper
1$^{1}/_{2}$	teaspoons dried basil
1	tablespoon dried oregano
4	dashes Tabasco sauce
$^{1}/_{4}$	cup grated Parmesan cheese
6	hamburger buns
2	cups grated Mozzarella cheese

❖ *P*reheat oven to 400 degrees. Brown ground beef in skillet, breaking meat up into fine pieces as it cooks; drain. Stir in pizza sauce, onion salt, garlic, salt, pepper, basil, oregano and Tabasco sauce. Add Parmesan cheese; stir until melted. Place meat mixture on bottoms only of hamburger buns; place on cookie sheet. Sprinkle Mozzarella cheese over top. Bake at 400 degrees for 3 minutes or until cheese melts. Replace tops; serve.

HOT, HOT BEANS

Servings: 15

1   lb. pork sausage
1   (16-oz.) can pork and beans
1   (16-oz.) can baby lima beans, drained
1   (16-oz.) can green beans, drained
1   (16-oz.) can yellow beans, drained
1   (16-oz.) can hot chili beans, drained
1   cup firmly packed brown sugar
1   (6-oz.) can tomato paste
1   (10.5-oz.) can tomato soup
1/2   cup barbecue sauce
3-4   slices bacon

❖ *P*reheat oven to 350 degrees. Brown and drain sausage. Combine all ingredients except barbecue sauce and bacon in a 5-quart casserole. Cover with sauce and place bacon strips on top. Bake at 350 degrees for 60 minutes.

CRUNCHY FUDGE BARS

Yield: 16 bars

1   cup butterscotch chips
1/2   cup peanut butter
4   cups rice cereal
1   cup semi-sweet chocolate chips
1/2   cup powdered sugar
2   tablespoons butter
1   tablespoon water

❖ *B*utter 8-inch square pan. Melt butterscotch chips with peanut butter in large saucepan over low heat. Stir until smooth; remove from heat. Stir in rice cereal until evenly coated. Press 1/2 of mixture into prepared pan; chill. In small saucepan, melt chocolate chips, sugar, butter and water over low heat until smooth. Spread over chilled mixture. Top with remaining rice mixture; chill. Cut into squares. Store in refrigerator.

This page has been underwritten through the generosity of MARGIE & JIM BIGGAR.

Menu

GIFT IDEAS

Irish Cream Liqueur
Butterscotch Rum Sauce
Swedish Nuts
Best Hot Fudge Sauce
Peanut Brittle
Kentucky Henry Baines Sauce
Caramel Popcorn
Pepper Jelly

IRISH CREAM LIQUEUR

Servings: 6-8

1³/₄ cups Irish whiskey

1 cup whipping cream

4 eggs

2 teaspoons instant coffee powder or granules

1 teaspoon vanilla

¹/₂ teaspoon almond extract

❖ Combine all ingredients in food processor or blender. Process until smooth. Store in refrigerator tightly covered up to 1 month.

BUTTERSCOTCH RUM SAUCE

Yield: 1 ¹/₃ cups

1 cup firmly packed brown sugar

¹/₄ cup light corn syrup

4 tablespoons unsalted butter
Pinch salt

¹/₂ cup whipping cream

1¹/₂ teaspoons vanilla

¹/₄ teaspoon fresh lemon juice

1¹/₂ tablespoons dark rum

¹/₂ cup coarsely chopped pecans

❖ Combine brown sugar, corn syrup, butter and salt in small saucepan. Cook over moderate heat, stirring until sugar is dissolved. Brush down sugar crystals from sides of pan with brush dipped in cold water. Boil undisturbed for 12 minutes or until mixture reaches 280 F. degrees. Remove from heat. Stir in cream, vanilla, lemon juice, rum and pecans. Serve warm or at room temperature.

SWEDISH NUTS

Yield: 3 1/2 cups

1 1/2   cups blanched almonds
2   cups walnut halves
2   egg whites
1   cup sugar
       Dash salt
4   tablespoons butter

❖ *P*reheat oven to 250 degrees. Spread almonds and walnuts on cookie sheet. Bake at 250 degrees until nuts are golden brown; cool. Beat egg whites until stiff peaks form. Fold in sugar and salt. Beat until stiff. Fold nuts into meringue. Preheat oven to 350 degrees. Place butter on jelly roll pan. Place pan in oven until butter is melted. Spread nut mixture over butter. Bake at 325 degrees for 30 minutes. Cool for a few minutes, then gently stir to mix up meringue so mixture glazes the nuts. Cool completely before breaking into pieces.

BEST HOT FUDGE SAUCE

Yield: 2 1/2 cups

1 1/2   oz. (1 1/2 squares) unsweetened chocolate
1/2   cup butter
1 1/3   cups sugar
1   (5-oz.) can evaporated milk
1   teaspoon vanilla
       Pinch salt

❖ *M*elt chocolate and butter in medium saucepan. Stir in sugar, milk, vanilla and salt. Bring to a boil; boil 1 minute. Serve hot or cold. Store in refrigerator.

PEANUT BRITTLE

Yield: 3 lbs.

2¼ cups sugar

1¼ cups light corn syrup

¾ cup water

2 lbs. raw peanuts

2 tablespoons butter

1 teaspoon baking soda

❖ Grease cookie sheet. In large saucepan, combine sugar, corn syrup and water over medium-high heat to a temperature of 240 degrees. Add peanuts and boil until mixture reaches 305 degrees. Remove from heat. Stir in butter and baking soda. Stir well; pour onto prepared cookie sheet. Cool; break into pieces.

KENTUCKY HENRY BAINES SAUCE

Yield: 20 servings

2 (12-oz.) bottles chili sauce

1 cup ketchup

2 (9-oz.) bottles chutney

3 tablespoons finely chopped walnuts

3 tablespoons finely chopped pickled onion

2 teaspoons dry mustard

1-3 tablespoons Tabasco sauce

❖ Combine all ingredients in food processor or blender. Process just until combined. Serve over cream cheese with assorted crackers.

CARAMEL POPCORN

Yield: 4 cups

$2/3$	cup popping corn
$1/4$	cup oil
$1/2$	cup butter or margarine
1	cup firmly packed brown sugar
$1/4$	cup white corn syrup
1	teaspoon salt
1	teaspoon baking soda

❖ *P*reheat oven to 300 degrees. Spray large roasting pan with non-stick vegetable spray. Pop corn in oil; pour into prepared pan. Melt butter in large saucepan. Add brown sugar, corn syrup and salt. Boil for 5 minutes. Remove from heat. Add baking soda and stir until frothy. Pour over popcorn and toss to coat. Bake at 300 degrees for 3 to 5 minutes; toss. Bake additional 3 to 5 minutes; remove from oven. Toss mixture; allow to set for 3 to 5 minutes. Break into small pieces. Be prepared to make a second batch - it disappears quickly!

PEPPER JELLY

Yield: 4 pints

1	cup (4-6) chopped green peppers
$1/4$	cup (2-3) Jalepeno peppers, cored, seeded and chopped
$6^{1/2}$	cups sugar
$1^{1/2}$	cups cider vinegar
6	oz. liquid pectin

❖ *C*ombine green peppers, Jalepeno peppers, vinegar and sugar in large saucepan. Bring to a boil; skim off froth. Remove from heat and let sit 20 minutes. Bring to a boil over medium heat, stirring constantly. Add pectin. Simmer for 5 minutes. Pour into sterilized jars and seal. Serve over Cheddar or cream cheese with assorted crackers as an appetizer. Also great on ham or chicken sandwiches.

BRUNCH SENSATION

Servings: 8

6 slices bread, toasted, buttered and crust removed

1 lb. mild pork sausage, cooked and drained

6 eggs, beaten

2 cups half-and-half

1 lb. grated Cheddar cheese

❖ *P*reheat oven to 350 degrees. Grease bottom of 9 x 13-inch pan. Lay bread slices in bottom of prepared pan. Spread sausage evenly over bread. Top with eggs and half-and-half. Sprinkle with Cheddar cheese. Bake at 350 degrees for 50 to 60 minutes.

DUTCH BABIES

Servings: 6-8

Pancake

1/3 cup butter

4 eggs, slightly beaten

1 cup milk

1 cup flour

1 teaspoon sugar

1/8 teaspoon nutmeg

2 tablespoons powdered sugar

Topping

2 cups sliced fruit (strawberries, bananas, peaches, blueberries)

1/2 cup firmly packed brown sugar

1/2 cup sour cream

❖ *P*ANCAKE: Preheat oven to 425 degrees. Melt butter in a 3-inch deep quiche pan or 2 (9-inch) glass pie pans. Combine eggs, milk, flour, sugar and nutmeg. Pour into prepared pan(s). Bake at 425 degrees for 20 minutes or until puffy. Sprinkle with powdered sugar during last few minutes of baking. Pancake will rise 4 to 5 inches on sides, and form a well in center.

TOPPING: Spoon fruit into center of pancake. Sprinkle with brown sugar and top with dollops of sour cream. Cut into wedges to serve.

NOTE: This pancake puffs dramatically when baked. You'll want to have everyone seated for a spectacular presentation.

POPPY SEED DRESSING

Servings: 8

3/4 cup sugar

1/3 cup vinegar

1 teaspoon dry mustard

1 teaspoon salt

1½ tablespoons grated onion

1 cup vegetable oil

1½ tablespoons poppy seeds

❖ *I*n food processor or blender, combine sugar, vinegar, mustard, salt and onion. Process until smooth. With machine running, pour oil slowly into mixture. Stir in poppy seeds. Serve with fresh fruit or with a salad of Bibb lettuce, sliced avocado and fresh strawberries.

CINNAMON MUFFINS

Yield: 12 muffins or 36 mini muffins

1/2 cup sugar

1/3 cup vegetable shortening

1 egg

1½ cups all-purpose flour

1½ teaspoons baking powder

1/2 teaspoon salt

1/4 teaspoon nutmeg

1/2 cup milk

1/2 cup butter, melted

1/2 cup sugar

1 teaspoon cinnamon

❖ *P*reheat oven to 350 degrees. Generously grease muffin cups. Do not use paper liners. Combine 1/2 cup sugar and shortening; add egg and blend until light and fluffy. Sift flour, baking powder, salt and nutmeg. Alternately add milk and dry ingredients. Fill muffin cups 2/3 full. Bake at 350 degrees for 20 to 25 minutes. Combine 1/2 cup sugar and cinnamon. While still warm, roll muffins in melted butter; coat with cinnamon-sugar mixture.

This page has been underwritten through the generosity of SUSAN & GREG ALTHANS.

FOOTBALL PARTY

Apricot Brandy Slush
Nippy Cheese Rounds
Sweet & Sour Mustard with Cheese Cubes
Barbecued Hot Dogs
Blackened Chicken Fingers with Yellow Salsa
Confetti Cabbage Slaw
Mint Chocolate Chip Cookies

NIPPY CHEESE ROUNDS

Yield: 48 appetizers

1   (8-oz.) pkg. cream cheese, softened

1   small onion, grated

14   drops Tabasco sauce

6   tablespoons mayonnaise

1   cup grated Parmesan cheese

1   loaf party rye bread

3/4-1   lb. bacon, cooked and crumbled

❖ Combine cream cheese, onion, Tabasco, mayonnaise and Parmesan cheese until smooth; chill. Preheat broiler. Spread cheese mixture on bread slices; top with bacon. Broil until bubbly.

APRICOT BRANDY SLUSH

Yield: 30 servings

2   cups boiling water

4   tea bags

1   (12-oz.) can frozen orange juice, thawed

1   (12-oz.) can frozen lemonade, thawed

1 3/4   cups sugar

2 1/4   cups apricot brandy

7   cups warm water

❖ Steep tea bags in 2 cups boiling water; cool. In very large bowl, combine cooled tea, orange juice, lemonade, sugar and apricot brandy. Stir in 7 cups warm water. Freeze mixture for 12 hours; stir before serving.

SWEET and SOUR MUSTARD

Yield: 2 cups

6 oz. dry mustard
1/2 teaspoon black pepper
1/4 teaspoon white pepper
1/4 teaspoon cayenne pepper
1/4 cup water
2 cups sugar
1 cup butter or margarine
1 1/2 cups vinegar
1 teaspoon salt
3 eggs, beaten

❖ Combine mustard, black pepper, white pepper and cayenne. Add enough water to make a smooth sticky paste. In a medium saucepan, combine sugar, butter, vinegar, salt and eggs. Heat to boiling; remove from heat. Add 1/4 cup of hot mixture to mustard paste. Stir until smooth. Repeat until all of the hot mixture has been incorporated. Return the mixture to saucepan. Bring to a boil, stirring for 3 to 5 minutes. Ladle into jars. Refrigerate.

BARBECUED HOT DOGS

Yield: 2 cups

Sauce
1 cup ketchup
1 cup water
1/2 cup chopped celery
2 tablespoons dried onion
1/4 cup firmly packed brown sugar
5 tablespoons Worcestershire sauce
1 tablespoon lemon juice
2 tablespoons vinegar
1 teaspoon prepared mustard

Hot dogs
Hot dog buns

❖ SAUCE: Combine all sauce ingredients in medium saucepan; simmer 20 minutes. Add hot dogs to sauce. Simmer 15 minutes or until heated through. Place hot dogs in buns. Top with sauce.

BLACKENED CHICKEN FINGERS with YELLOW SALSA

Yield: 12-18 pieces

Yellow Salsa

1/2	cup chopped yellow tomato
1/4	cup finely chopped honeydew melon
1/4	cup finely chopped cucumber, peeled and seeded
1/2	small Jalepeno pepper, minced and seeded
2	teaspoons chopped cilantro
2	teaspoons fresh lime juice
1/2	teaspoon ground coriander
	Salt and white pepper, to taste

Chicken Fingers

3/4	cup unsalted butter
1/4	cup fresh lemon juice
1	tablespoon dried thyme
1	tablespoon dried basil
3	teaspoons freshly ground black pepper
1	teaspoon paprika
1/4	teaspoon cayenne pepper
	Season and salt, to taste
3	whole chicken breasts, skinned, boned and cut into 3 x 1-inch strips

❖ YELLOW SALSA: Combine all salsa ingredients; chill.

CHICKEN FINGERS: Melt butter in medium saucepan. Stir in lemon juice, thyme, basil, black pepper, paprika, cayenne pepper and seasoned salt. Dip chicken in butter mixture, coating thoroughly. Place on plate and chill for 1 hour. Reserve butter mixture. Heat cast iron skillet over high heat until a drop of water sizzles. Place chicken strips in pan, cooking 1 to 2 minutes on each side to blacken. Do not crowd pan. Remove to platter. Serve with Yellow Salsa.

NOTE: The trick to "blackening" chicken is very cold meat and a very hot pan. A cast iron skillet is essential.

CONFETTI CABBAGE SLAW

Servings: 6-8

Dressing

2 egg yolks

1 tablespoon curry powder

4 tablespoons orange juice concentrate

1/8-1/4 teaspoon hot sauce

2 tablespoons Dijon mustard

2/3 cup vegetable oil

Salad

1 medium head cabbage, thinly sliced

1 cup frozen green peas, thawed

1 small red pepper, cut into julienne strips

3 green onions, thinly sliced

1/4 cup grated carrot

1/4 cup minced fresh Italian parsley

1/3 cup salted, roasted peanuts, chopped

❖ *D*RESSING: Place egg yolks, curry powder, orange juice, hot sauce and mustard in food processor or blender. With machine running, add oil in a slow steady stream. Process until thick and smooth.

SALAD: Combine all salad ingredients in large glass bowl. Toss with a scant 3/4 cup of dressing. Refrigerate overnight.

MINT CHOCOLATE COOKIES

Yield: 2 1/2 dozen

1 (10-oz.) pkg. mint flavored semi-sweet chocolate chips

1/2 cup margarine or butter flavored shortening

1/4 cup sugar

1/2 cup firmly packed dark brown sugar

1 egg

1 teaspoon vanilla

1 1/4 cups all-purpose flour

1 teaspoon baking soda

2/3 cup chopped pecans

❖ *P*reheat oven to 350 degrees. Grease cookie sheets. In small saucepan melt 3/4 cup of chocolate chips over medium heat; set aside. Beat margarine, sugar, brown sugar, egg and vanilla until smooth. Stir in melted chocolate; beat until smooth. Add flour, baking soda, remaining chocolate chips and pecans; stir until smooth. Drop by teaspoonfuls onto prepared cookie sheets. Bake at 350 degrees for 8 minutes.

Menu

MEXICAN NITE

Margaritas
Arizona Salsa
Guacamole
Mexican Lasagna
Sour Cream Enchiladas

MARGARITAS

Servings: 3

6 oz. frozen limeade concentrate, thawed
6 oz. tequila
Ice cubes

❖ *F*ill blender container with ice. Add limeade and tequila. Blend until frothy. Add water as necessary to blend. Freeze in blender container. Margaritas may be frozen from 2 to 4 weeks.

STEVEN KERR

ARIZONA SALSA

Yield: 3 cups

2 cloves garlic
1 can (28-oz.) whole tomatoes
1 bunch fresh cilantro
6 green onions, cleaned and trimmed

1 teaspoon dried crushed red pepper
Salt and pepper, to taste

❖ *P*lace garlic in food processor or blender. Process until minced. Add remaining ingredients. Process mixture until just blended. Refrigerate one hour before serving. Serve with warm tortilla chips, margaritas or beer.

analysis does not include the tortilla chips

Guard for the Cleveland Cavaliers

GUACAMOLE

Yield: 3 cups

3   large ripe avocados, peeled and pitted
2   tablespoons minced onion
2   tablespoons lemon juice
1   clove garlic, minced
4   drops Tabasco sauce
1   teaspoon salt
3/4 teaspoon chili powder
1/4 cup sour cream
1/3 cup prepared salsa
1   medium tomato, peeled, seeded and chopped
1/2 cup mayonnaise

❖ *In* food processor, combine 2 avocados, onion, lemon juice, garlic, Tabasco sauce, salt and chili powder. Process until pureed. Pour into large bowl. Finely chop remaining avocado. Stir into pureed mixture. Stir in sour cream, salsa and tomatoes. Spread mayonnaise over mixture to seal. (This prevents discoloration.) Chill. Before serving, blend mayonnaise into mixture.

MEXICAN LASAGNE

Servings: 4

1   lb. ground beef
1   medium onion, chopped
1   clove garlic, minced
1   (8-oz.) can tomato sauce
1   (4-oz.) can sliced ripe olives, drained
1   tablespoon chili powder
1   teaspoon salt
1/4 teaspoon pepper
6   flour tortillas, buttered
2   cups shredded Cheddar cheese

❖ *P*reheat oven to 400 degrees. Brown ground beef, onion and garlic in large skillet; drain. Add tomato sauce, olives, chili powder, salt and pepper. In round 2-quart casserole, alternately layer 2 tortillas, 1/3 of meat sauce and 1/2 cup Cheddar cheese. Sprinkle remaining 1/2 cup cheese over top. Cover and bake at 400 degrees for 25 minutes. Uncover and allow to stand at room temperature 5 minutes before cutting into wedges.

SOUR CREAM ENCHILADAS

Servings: 12

White Sauce

1	tablespoon flour
1	tablespoon butter
$1/2$	cup milk

Tomato Sauce

$1/2$	cup chopped onion
1	large clove garlic, minced
2	tablespoons olive oil
1	tablespoons all-purpose flour
1	tablespoon chili powder
$1/2$	teaspoon dried oregano
$1/2$	teaspoon ground cumin
1	teaspoon salt
1	cup tomato paste
1	cup water

Enchiladas

$1/4$	cup vegetable oil
12	large flour tortillas
16	oz. shredded Monterrey Jack cheese
1	(4-oz.) can whole green chilies, cut into strips
	Salt and pepper
$1^1/2$	cups prepared sauce
$1/2$	cup white sauce
$2^1/2$	cups sour cream

❖ WHITE SAUCE: Melt butter in small saucepan over low heat. Add flour and stir 'til bubbly. Whisk in milk. Stir until thickened.

❖ TOMATO SAUCE: In large saucepan, cook onion and garlic in oil until transparent. Add flour and cook for 1 minute. Add remaining tomato sauce ingredients. Simmer 20 minutes. Yield: 2 cups.

ENCHILADAS: Preheat oven to 350 degrees. Generously grease a 13 x 9-inch pan. Heat oil in medium skillet. Dip tortillas in hot oil; drain on paper towel. In center of each tortilla, place $1/4$ cup cheese, $1/12$ of green chili strips, salt, pepper and 2 tablespoons of prepared tomato sauce. Roll up and place seam-side-down in prepared pan. Repeat for all tortillas. Combine sour cream and white sauce; pour over enchiladas. Top with remaining cheese. Bake at 350 degrees for 30 minutes or until bubbly and cheese is melted.

POLO BUFFET

Caper Dip

Turkey Paté

Polo Punch

Greek Potato Salad

Dinner Party Beef

Cream Cheese Mousse Crepes
with Raspberry Grand Marnier Sauce

CAPER DIP

Yield: 2 cups

1/2   cup sour cream

1   cup mayonnaise

1/8   teaspoon curry powder

1/4   teaspoon salt

1   tablespoon grated onion

1   teaspoon lemon juice

1/2   teaspoon Worcestershire sauce

2   tablespoons chopped fresh parsley

2   tablespoons capers, washed, drained and dried

❖ Combine all ingredients except capers. In small bowl, mash capers; stir into sour cream mixture. Chill two hours. Serve with assorted crudites.

TURKEY PATÉ

Servings: 6-8

1   cup cubed cooked turkey breast

1   teaspoon anchovy paste

1/2   cup butter

1   tablespoon grated onion

2   teaspoon lemon juice

1/4   teaspoon salt

1/8   teaspoon white pepper

1-2   dashes Tabasco sauce

❖ Place all ingredients into food processor or blender. Process until smooth. Chill. Serve on thin toast, French bread or thin slices of pumpernickel.

POLO PUNCH

Servings: 24

4   (8-oz.) cans frozen orange juice, thawed

1   (12-oz.) can frozen lemonade, thawed

2   (2-liter) bottles ginger ale

1   liter bottle Canadian Mist

❖ Combine all ingredients in large punch bowl. Serve.

GREEK POTATO SALAD

Servings: 8-10

Dressing

- 1 teaspoon beaten egg yolk
- 2 tablespoons red wine vinegar
- 1 tablespoon fresh lemon juice
- 1 teaspoon Dijon mustard
- 1/2 cup olive oil
- 3/4 cup vegetable oil

Salad

- 3 lbs. red new potatoes, washed
  Kosher salt
  Freshly ground black pepper
- 1/2 cup chopped fresh parsley
- 1/3 cup chopped green onions
- 3 tablespoons chopped fresh dill
- 1/2 cup sliced hearts of palm

❖ DRESSING: Combine egg yolk, vinegar, lemon juice and mustard in food processor or blender. Combine olive oil and vegetable oil. With machine running, add oil in slow steady stream. Process until thickened.

SALAD: Boil or steam potatoes until tender but not soft. Rinse in cold water. Cut into bite-sized wedges. Toss with small amount of dressing. Chill. Add salt, pepper, parsley, green onions, dill and hearts of palm. Toss with additional dressing. Garnish with fresh dill sprigs and cherry tomato halves.

DINNER PARTY BEEF

Servings: 6-8

Marinade

- 1/2 cup Dijon mustard
- 3 tablespoons dry sherry
- 3 tablespoons soy sauce
- 1 tablespoon vegetable oil
- 3 tablespoons firmly packed brown sugar
- 1 clove garlic, finely minced
- 1/2 teaspoon Tabasco sauce

- 1 (2-lb.) London broil or flank steak

❖ Combine all marinade ingredients. Place London broil in large plastic bag with seal. Pour marinade mixture over meat; seal tightly. Refrigerate 24 hours, turning bag frequently. Prepare grill. Remove meat from marinade. Reserve marinade for basting. Grill meat over medium coals for 10 minutes (medium rare), turning once; baste frequently. Slice crossgrain into 1/4 to 1/3-inch slices.

NOTE: Marinade may be doubled. Reserve 1/2 of marinade for a "pouring/dipping" sauce for the meat.

CREAM CHEESE MOUSSE CREPES with RASPBERRY GRAND MARNIER SAUCE

Servings: 10-12 crepes

Crepes

1/2	cup sifted all-purpose flour
2	eggs
1 1/2	tablespoons sugar
3/4	cup milk
	Dash salt
1/4	teaspoon vanilla
1 1/2	teaspoons Grand Marnier

Filling

1/2	cup whipping cream
2	tablespoons powdered sugar
1	(8-oz.) pkg. cream cheese, softened
1	tablespoon super fine sugar
1/2	teaspoon Grand Marnier
1/4	cup whipping cream
	Dash cinnamon
1	teaspoon vanilla
1/4	teaspoon finely grated orange rind

Sauce

1	tablespoon water
1	teaspoon arrowroot or cornstarch
1	(10-oz.) pkg. frozen sweetened raspberries
1/4	cup Grand Marnier

❖ CREPES: Combine all crepe ingredients, beating with a rotary beater until smooth. Refrigerate several hours to thicken. Use 2 to 3 tablespoons batter for each crepe. Cook crepes in lightly greased skillet. Cook on one side only until light brown. Turn crepes out onto waxed paper.

FILLING: Beat 1/2 cup whipping cream and powdered sugar until thick; refrigerate. Beat cream cheese and sugar until smooth. Gradually add 1/4 cup whipping cream, Grand Marnier, cinnamon, vanilla and orange rind. Stir until smooth. Fold in remaining whipped cream. Divide filling between crepes and roll crepes. Refrigerate.

SAUCE: Combine water and arrowroot. In small saucepan, bring raspberries to a boil. Add dissolved arrowroot mixture and cook until sauce is clear; strain. Add Grand Marnier and cool. Serve each crepe with a few tablespoons of sauce.

BRUNCH

Eggs Olé
Hot Fruit Compote
Gooey Buns

EGGS OLÉ

Servings: 8

6 large eggs, beaten
1 (12-oz.) can evaporated milk
1 lb. Colby/Monterey Jack cheese, shredded
1 (4-oz.) can chopped green chilies, drained

❖ *P*reheat oven to 350 degrees. Combine eggs and milk. Layer 1/2 of green chilies in bottom of an 8 x 8-inch pan. Sprinkle 1/2 of cheese over top. Repeat layers. Pour egg mixture over top. Bake at 350 degrees for 30 minutes.

HOT FRUIT COMPOTE

Servings: 6-8

1/4 cup butter
3/4 cup powdered sugar
1 teaspoon cornstarch
2 teaspoons grated orange rind
1/3 cup orange juice
2 tablespoons lemon juice
1 (20-oz.) can pineapple chunks, well drained
1 (11-oz.) can mandarin oranges, well drained
1 (16-oz.) can sliced peaches, well drained
1 (16-oz.) can sliced pears, well drained
10 Maraschino cherries

❖ *I*n chafing dish or large saucepan, combine butter, sugar, cornstarch, orange rind, orange juice and lemon juice. Cook over low heat until slightly thickened. Stir in fruit. Heat just until fruit is warm. Serve with a dollop of whipped cream, if desired.

NOTE: To make ahead, cover and refrigerate mixture just after fruit is added. Preheat oven to 350 degrees. Bake for 30 to 45 minutes or just until fruit is heated through.

GOOEY BUNS

Yield: 24 rolls

Dough

1	pkg. active dry yeast
2	tablespoons sugar
1/4	cup warm water (105 degrees F. to 115 degrees F.)
1	tablespoon salt
1/4	cup sugar
2	cups hot water
1/3	cup vegetable shortening
1	egg, lightly beaten
6	cups all-purpose flour

Sauce

3/4	cup butter
1 3/4	cups firmly packed brown sugar
3	tablespoons half-and-half
1 3/4	cups chopped pecans

Topping

3/4	cup melted butter
1/2	cup sugar
1/4	cup ground cinnamon

❖ *D*OUGH: Dissolve yeast and 2 tablespoons sugar in 1/4 cup warm water. Allow to stand for 5 minutes. Dissolve salt and 1/4 cup sugar in 2 cups hot water. Add shortening and mix until shortening is melted. Add egg, 2 cups flour and yeast mixture. Beat until smooth. Add 2 more cups flour, working dough until moistened. Add remaining 2 cups flour and work dough until smooth. Place dough in greased bowl, turning to coat all sides. Cover with plastic wrap and let rise in refrigerator overnight.

In large saucepan, melt 3/4 cup butter. Add brown sugar and half-and-half; simmer. Pour into 2 (9 x 13-inch) pans. Sprinkle with pecans. Remove dough from refrigerator; divide in half. On floured surface, roll each dough half into a 12 x 8-inch rectangle. Spread with 3/4 cup melted butter. Combine sugar and cinnamon; sprinkle over dough. Starting from long side, roll each rectangle jelly roll style. Slice into 1-inch pieces. Place cut-side-down in prepared pans. Cover and let rise until doubled in size. Bake in preheated 350 degree oven for 20 to 25 minutes.

This page has been underwritten through the generosity of MR. & MRS. ARTHUR J. ALTHANS II.

MENU

ADULT BIRTHDAY PARTY

Martini Madness
Hot Clam Dip
Herbed Biscuits
Salad with Blue Cheese Dressing
White Chili

MARTINI MADNESS

1¹/₄	**cups vodka**
¹/₄	**cups Lillet Blanc (French aperitif)**
2	**(2-inch) strips orange peel**

❖ *O*ne day in advance, mix vodka and Lillet Blanc. Pour into a freezer container. Add orange peel and stir. Freeze, covered for at least 12 hours. Remove orange peel; reserve. Pour martinis into 2 well chilled martini glasses. Twist the orange strips and ignite before dropping into martini glasses.

HOT CLAM DIP

Servings: 4

¹/₄	**cup butter**
¹/₄	**cup finely chopped onion**
1	**(6 ¹/₂-oz.) can minced clams, drained**
¹/₄	**cup ketchup**
2	**tablespoons Worcestershire sauce**
6	**dashes Tabasco sauce**
1¹/₂	**cups Velveeta or Olde English cheese**

❖ *M*elt butter in small saucepan over low heat. Add onion and clams. Saute over medium heat for 5 minutes. Add ketchup, Worcestershire sauce, and Tabasco sauce; stirring constantly. Add cheese and stir over medium heat until melted. Serve hot.

HERBED BISCUITS

Servings: 4

3   tablespoons butter
1   tablespoon minced onion
1   teaspoon dried dill
1   teaspoon poppy seeds
1   (10-ct.) pkg. buttermilk biscuits
1/4 cup grated Parmesan cheese

❖ *P*reheat oven to 400 degrees. Melt butter in 8-inch round cake pan. Sprinkle onion, dill and poppy seeds in bottom of prepared pan. Cut each biscuit into 4 pieces. Place biscuit pieces in bag with Parmesan cheese; shake to coat. Place in pan. Bake at 400 degrees for 15 to 18 minutes or until golden brown.

BLUE CHEESE SALAD DRESSING

Yield: 2 1/2 cups

1   cup mayonnaise
2/3 cup sour cream
2   tablespoons chopped onion
2   tablespoons vinegar
2/3 cup crumbled blue cheese
    Salt and pepper, to taste
    Parsley flakes

❖ *C*ombine mayonnaise, sour cream, onion and vinegar in food processor or blender at low speed. Add 1/2 cup blue cheese, salt, pepper and parsley flakes (if desired). Process until well combined. Stir in remaining blue cheese; chill.

WHITE CHILI

Servings: 6

1   tablespoon vegetable oil
1   medium onion, chopped
1-2 cloves garlic, minced
1   (12-oz.) can white corn, drained
1   (15- oz.) can white kidney beans, drained
2   whole chicken breasts, skinned, boned and cubed
1   (15-oz.) can garbanzo beans, drained
1   (4-oz.) can chopped green chilies, drained
1 1/2 cups chicken stock
     Hot pepper sauce, to taste
6   oz. shredded Monterey Jack cheese

❖ *P*reheat oven to 350 degrees. In small skillet, saute onion and garlic in oil until tender. In 2 1/2-quart casserole, combine onion mixture, corn, kidney beans, chicken, garbanzo beans and chilies. Cover and bake at 350 degrees for 50 to 60 minutes or until chicken is tender. Remove from oven. Stir in chicken stock and hot pepper sauce. Bake additional 20 minutes or until hot and bubbly. Sprinkle cheese on top of servings.

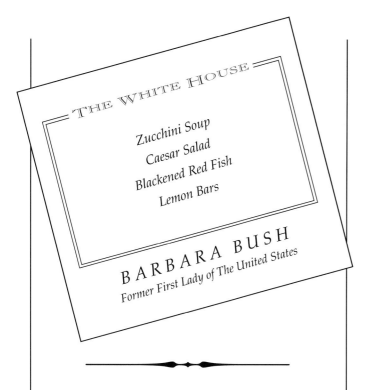

THE WHITE HOUSE

Zucchini Soup
Caesar Salad
Blackened Red Fish
Lemon Bars

BARBARA BUSH
Former First Lady of The United States

CAESAR SALAD

Servings: 8

2-3	cloves garlic, quartered
1/2	cup olive oil
4	cups 1/4-inch fresh bread cubes
4	quarts assorted lettuce greens
1	cup grated Parmesan cheese
1/2	cup crumbled blue cheese
1	teaspoon salt
1/2	teaspoon pepper
1/4	cup olive oil
1	egg
7	tablespoons lemon juice
2	tablespoons Worcestershire sauce

❖ Soak garlic in olive oil at room temperature overnight. Preheat oven to 300 degrees. Place bread cubes in shallow pan. Toast at 300 degrees for 30 minutes or until golden brown, turning occasionally with a fork. Cool; wrap tightly.

In large bowl, sprinkle lettuce greens with Parmesan cheese, blue cheese, salt and pepper. Add 1/4 cup olive oil. In small bowl, combine egg, lemon juice and Worcestershire sauce. Pour over salad and toss. Remove garlic from oil mixture. Toss croutons with oil mixture. (Do this at the last moment so that croutons do not get soggy.) Add croutons to salad; toss.

ZUCCHINI SOUP

Servings: 6-8

1	lb. unpeeled zucchini, cleaned and chopped
2	tablespoons shallots, chopped (onion or leeks may be used)
1	clove garlic, minced
2	tablespoons butter or margarine
1 3/4	cups chicken broth
1	teaspoon curry powder
1/2	teaspoon salt
1/2	cup cream

❖ In heavy skillet, saute zucchini, shallots and garlic in butter. Cook for 10 to 20 minutes until translucent, stirring occasionally. Place vegetables, chicken broth, curry powder and salt into blender or food processor. Process until smooth. Add cream. Heat and serve hot with croutons or chill and serve cold with chives.

BLACKENED RED FISH

Servings: 8

Seasonings

1	tablespoon paprika
2½	teaspoons salt
1	teaspoon onion powder
1	teaspoon cayenne pepper
1	teaspoon garlic powder
¾	teaspoon white pepper
¾	teaspoon black pepper
½	teaspoon dried thyme
½	teaspoon dried oregano
3	lbs. redfish fillets, ½ to ¾-inch thick
	Melted butter or margarine

❖ SEASONINGS: Combine all seasoning ingredients.

Dip fish in melted butter; coat well with seasoning mixture. Preheat cast iron skillet on high until very hot. Cook fish fillets 2 minutes; turn and cook 1 minute. This dish is very smoky to prepare; it cooks well outside on a grill or campstove.

LEMON BARS

For the lemon lovers of America

Yield: 48

1	cup butter or margarine, softened
2	cups powdered sugar
2	cups all-purpose flour
4	teaspoons fresh lemon juice
	Rind of 2 lemons, grated
4	eggs, well beaten
2	cups sugar
1	teaspoon baking powder
¼	cup all-purpose flour
1	cup shredded coconut (optional)

❖ *P*reheat oven to 350 degrees. Combine butter, sugar and flour. Batter will be stiff. Spread into 10 x 15-inch pan. Bake at 350 degrees for 15 minutes or until light golden brown. Cool. Combine lemon juice, lemon rind, eggs, sugar, baking powder, flour and coconut, if desired. Pour over base. Bake at 350 degrees for 35 minutes. Cool; cut into bars.

COOKBOOK STEERING COMMITTEES

1991-1992
*BONNIE FEMEC**
*MARCIE QUA**
SUSAN O. ALTHANS
SUSAN ANTON
SUE BALOG
MARILYN BUTLER
LAUREL R. CARABOOLAD
MELISSA DRANE
JAN GOTSCHALL
MARGARET ANN GIBSON
BETTYANN GORMAN
BARBARA GRANO
HELEN GREENLEAF
CAROL HOLDER
BARBARA KAMEN
MADELYN KOLTCZ
PAT KRASSEN
DAWN LAMARCO
CHRIS LAMBERT
KIM LANSDOWNE
CYNTHIA LEHMAN
GINGER LUCAS
JAN MANNING
SUE MCKAY

CAROLYN NEWMAN
MARY PATERNITE
MARY CLARE PATTERSON
PATTI PERLMUTER
ROBBI RIGNEY
JACKIE SAFIER
DEE P. SAMUELSON
PEG SMITH
LEE ANNE STUEBER
JANE TEMPLE
ANNA WARREN
VALERIE WEAVER

1992-1993
*BONNIE FEMEC**
*CAROLYN NEWMAN**
MARGARET ANN GIBSON
DAWN LAMARCO
CHRISTINE LAMBERT
CATHLEEN LANE
DEBBIE MANDT
MARY CLARE PATTERSON
AUDREY STARK
JANE TEMPLE
ADRIENNE WILSON

1993-1994
*ADRIENNE WILSON**
*ELISA BUDOFF**
KATHLEEN CARVIN
KRISTIN HORN
DEBBIE MANDT
LAURA SAMPSON
BETSY WANAMAKER
JOANNE ZETTL

1994-1995
*DEBBIE BEDELL**
*ADRIENNE WILSON**
ROSEMARY DOWNING
ELIZABETH FIORDALIS
BARBARA GRANO
HELEN GREENLEAF
DEBBIE HERMANN
CATHLEEN LANE
PATTI PADDOCK
VANESSA PASIADIS
ELIZABETH PETREQUIN
LEE ANNE STUEBER

*Committee Co-Chairs

TESTERS

APPETIZERS
CHRIS JONES*
Jane Cooper
Rosemary Downing
Vanessa Pasiadis
Mary Clare Patterson
Kim Ramey
Denise Vinton
Marcie Qua
Valerie Weaver

BREADS
SUSAN CULLMAN*
Jonetta Kapusta
Gerilyn Keeney
Jan Manning
Julia Sullivan

CELEBRITY RECIPES
BETTYANN GORMAN*
Margee Brennan
Barbara Kamen
Cynthia Lehman
Susie Ostrowski
Chris Vilas

DESSERTS
KATHY BEDER*
Jennifer Belt
Heather Crampton
Susan Emory
Amy Fischer
Sharon Fruchey
Kathy Gillen
Judy Gulling
Melissa Johnston
Susan Meier
Ann Saunders
Sharon Sobol
Cindy Victor

CELEBRATIONS
CAROLYN NEWMAN*
Margaret Ann Gibson
Odette Hankins
Iris Harvie
Debbie Hermann
Debbie Kuehm
Mary Susan Lyon
Buster Oldenburg
Betsy Stueber

FISH
ADRIENNE OTIS*
Susan Althans
Nancy Liber
Karen Murgiano
Marcie Qua
Julia Sullivan

MEATS & POULTRY
ELLEN LUTJEN*
Shannon Callewart
Bobbie Donelson
Dee Dee Gaul
Bonnie Gepfert
Mary Margaret
Lawrence
Nancy Malangoni
Marty Meserole
Trisha Pavey
Cathy Pleasant
Erika Reale
Gretchen Russell
Betty Seymour
Lynn Wood

**PASTA, RICE
& VEGETABLES**
SHARON WIANT*
LAUREL CARABOOLAD*
Cheryl Cameron
Sue Froman
Tina McGuire
Susan McNamara
Wendy Murphy
Patti Perlmuter
Meredith Wellman

RESTAURANTS
Helen Greenleaf
Kim Lansdowne

SOUPS & SALADS
SUE MCKAY*
Mary Ann Cooper
Laura Sterkel Grant
Pamela Mellor
Janet Nelson
Karen Porcelli
Georgianna Roberts

*Denotes Section Chairs

RESTAURANT & CELEBRITY RECIPE CONTRIBUTORS

The Junior League of Cleveland, Inc. wishes to express its appreciation to the celebrities and Cleveland restaurants who contributed recipes to this book.

Baricelli Inn

Hyde Park Grill

Massimo da Milano

Players Pizza & Pasta Restaurant

The Ritz - Carlton

Sfuzzi's Restaurant

Josephine R. Abady

Kenneth Frances Bates

Erma Bombeck

Brian Brennan

Barbara Bush

Tim Conway

Joel Grey

Bob Hope

Steven Kerr

Bernie Kosar

Mr. & Mrs. Jahja Ling

Dennis Nahat

Susan Orlean

Wolf Utian

Janet Voinovich

George Voinovich

Robert J. White, M.D.

Tamera White

Ambassador & Mrs. Milton Wolf

RECIPE CONTRIBUTORS

Martha Aarons
Sandy Abookire
Barbara B. Aggers
Susan O. Althans
Cleo E. Anton
Mrs. P.E. Anton
Susan Anton
Thalia E. Anton
Lois Armington
Debra D. Arthur
Margaret Y. Atwater

Elizabeth H. Bacon
Margot F. Baldwin
Susan A. Balog
Sarah M. Barber
Cindy Barker-Ruddock
Julianne T. Barry
Cynthia Bassett
Kenneth F. Bates
Kathleen Bauer
Katherine X. Beder
Jeanie Belhobek
Jennifer Belt
Judy Belt
Pam Bennett
Cheryl T. Berrodin
Sherry Whay Bieganski
Dennis Bikum
Liz Blunden
Beth Boles
Sue Bonhomme
Rebecca Borden
R. Kevin Borowiak
Ann Elizabeth Boughner
Ann J. Bowdish
Martha W. Boyer
Martha H. Bradford
Karen Brasdovich
Nancy Breech
Marjorie A. Brianas
Mary K. Broadbent
Sharon Brockman
Natalie Brown
Pam Burdett
Carson D. Burke
Holly H. Burke
Marilyn Butler
Shannon Callewart
Cheryl Cameron
Linda Campbell
Nancy Campbell
Laurel R. Caraboolad
S. Lynn Carlson
Karen A. Carmen
Colleen A. Carmigiano
Nancy C. Carpenter
Mrs. William L. Cassidy
Carol Castle
Connie Cavalier
Ann F. Champlin
Kathleen Nott Chimples
Gerry Chittock
Nancy Clark
Patty Cleary
Barbara C. Clements
Nancy Cockley
Kathy Coleman
Leslie Coleman

Victoria Collin
Sue Conant
Tracy Coneglio
Sally K. Conley
Marie A. Consolo
Pamela P. Cooley
Mary Ann Cooper
Margot James Copeland
Elizabeth F. Cotter
Monica Cronin
Cynthia K. Curtin
Jo Curva
John Curva
Laure Nau Curva
Sara G. Cutting
Carol Daniel
Monica Jorden Daniel
Anthea R. Daniels
Diane P. Daniels
E. Daniels
Kay S. Daugherty
Debra J. Davis
Anne DeLozier
Mary Lou DePolo
Mary Dickes
Roberta P. Donelson
Judy Dowd
Melissa Drane
Megan M. Driver
Karla Dulic
Susan Dwyer
Lorianne Dyke
Pamela Edlund
Susan Emory
Diane Euchenhofer
Maryann Falco
Carol Falendar
Katherine Fardney
Bonnie L. Femec
Amy B. Fischer
Carol T. Forbes
Signe W. Forbes
Judith Foss
Stacy Frank
Sandra Jeanne Fridrich
Mari Fritzsche-Poss
Claudia S. Fulton
Susan Gavazzi
Margario Geltman
Judith S. Gibbs
Margaret Ann Gibson
Jan Gift
Kathy Gillen
Barbara S. Gordon
Barbara Grano
Laura Sterkel Grant
Joanne Greene

Helen Greenleaf
Miriam J. Greeve
Wilbur S. Gregory II
Donna Greiner
Joan Gretter
Linda Griffin
Eileen H. Guffin
Katherine A. Haag
Joie S. Haddad
Betty Haffey
Jane Hagan
Nancy Hale
Diane Hanick
Odette M. Hankins
Susan E. Hanna
Debra Harrington
Janice Xinakes Harris
Margit Harris
Martha M. Hartland
Janice H. Hassink
Hildy Hefferman
Lynn M. Heisler
Marjorie A. Heller
John A. Hellman
Lois S. Helnick
Sofia Henry
Roberta Herman
Debbie S. Hermann
Cinda Herndon-King
Skipper Weir Hewlett
Michele P. Hill
Sara S. Hill
Marilyn Hofford
Holly W. Holcomb
Carol Holder
Sandra D. Holmes
Janalee James
Stephanie Jarrett
Tracy Jensen
Christine D. Jones
Sherry Jones
Juanita Juarez
Barbara Schenkelberg Kamen
Laura Kappas
Lollie Kasulones
Gerilyn Keeney
Peggy Kellermeyer
Douglas Kelly
Nancy Kelly
Catherine Kilbane
Elizabeth White King
Mary Cassidy Kleinman
Mary Klonaris
Mary Kohe
Margaret E. Kohn
Sandra Kiely Kolb

Madelyn Koltcz
Anne Marie Kopp
Christine Kramer
Kathleen Kramer
Patricia Meyer Krassen
Karen Kraus
Deborah G. Kuehm
Sharon Kuhn
Peggy Kundtz
Patricia Kunkel
Joneta J. Kupusta
Lynne LaFalce
Dawn LaMarco
Gail LaMarco
L. Christine Lambert
Cathleen Lane
Kim Lansdowne
Venera Lawicki
Bonnie Lawson
Abigail LeMay
Cynthia Lehman
Ginny Lehman
Carol Leslie
Bonnie M. Lewis
Nancy Liber
Corby Locke
Donna Luprion
Ellen Lutjen
Mary Susan Lyon
Pamela Macko
Patrice L. Maddox
Connie Malagoni
Nancy Malangoni
Sheila M. Manley
Nancy Marana
Janet Marshall
Barbara S. Martien
Eloise Mason
Donna Marie Mastropitre
Kyle Mauroth
Shirley May
Janet M. McClurkin
Linda L. McCormick
Mary E. McGinnis
Diane H. McKay
Sue McKay
Betty McWilliams
Pamela Mellor
Marjorie Mertz
Linda H. Meyer
Claire Scott Miller
Kathy Miller
Mary R. Miller
Pat Moore
Marilyn Morris

Mary Ellen Morrissey
Kay Muller
Karen Murgiano
Judith E. Musser
Gail Nackel
Debra Nail
Cynthia Campbell Nairn
S. Bruce Nairn
Dee Dee Nemeth
Carolyn A. Newman
Helen B. Newman
Cindy Newton
Effie Nikolaou
Shirley Nook
Frances Norwick
Maureen O'Malley
Kathleen O'Neil
Liz O'Neil
Ann Lynn Odolo
Katherine Kelley Ohlrich
Buster Oldenburg
Chloe Oldenburg
Sylvia Oliver
Victoria Oney
Cindy Onorato
Susan M. Ostrowski
Judy Pace
Patti Paddock
Vanessa M. Pasiadis
Mary J. Paternite
Virginia E. Paterson
Mary Clare Patterson
Warren D. Patterson
Cynthia Paul
Kathleen A. Pease
Patti Perlmuter
June Petrequin
Catherine Pleasant
Karen A. Porcelli
Mary N. Powell
Elizabeth F. Pratt
Martha F. Qua
Martha M. Qua
Stephen M. Qua II
Erika Reale
Jane Redinger
Ann Reece
Caroline Reich
Katherine Rieger
Kathryn K. Riego
Dolly Riffle
Linda Riffle
Linda Roberto
Ellen M. Roberts
Georgianna Roberts

Katherine Rockman
Marlene Rose
Doddie Rossman
Michelle Rowse
Mary Ann Ruggles
Diane Ruppel-Petrone
Gretchen S. Russell
Lindsey Russo
Janine H. Rybka
Pat Rydquist
JoAnn S. Salon
Diann G. Scaravilli
Joyce E. Schanz
M. Elizabeth Schiau
Judith R. Schramm
Nancy D. Schrank
Sally Schulze
Linda Milan Shatteen
Shirley Shiffman
Gloria Wells Simms
Randice Simon
Mary Lou Slife
Becky Smythe
Leslie Sondberg
Jeanne S. Speck
Donna Stadnik
Christine Sterkel
Georgia Stonehill
Karen Strang
Suzanne Stratton-Crooke
Holly C. Strauch
Gerald A. Stueber
Jean Stueber
Lee Anne Speck Stueber
Janet Sukenaga
Lisa L. Sullivan
Leslie Sundberg
Molly B. Sussen
Bernadene Swaney
Martin A. Tabone
Judith Taimzing
Julie D. Tamarkin
Catherine Tasse
Eva P. Taylor
Laurie Taylor
Jane Temple
Synthia S. Terhune
Sally Terrell
Sandra Billow Teschler
Marcie Thompson
Martha P. Thompson
Lisa Tidyman
Debbie Timen
Maryellen S. Tobias
Maria Tobin

Merlene Treuhaft
Judith Kaminski Tuinzing
Lisa L. Tutino
Thomas E. Usher
Judy McGrath Van Hecke
Patricia C. Van Hecke
Cindy Victor
Denise Vinton
Kathleen Visconsi
Chris Von Beck
Elizabeth Wagner
LaVonne Waller
Susan S. Wallbridge
LaVonne Waller
Nancy Wamsley
Betsy Wanamaker
Phyliss M. Wands
Mary Tiberi Warner
Anna A. Warren
Betty Lou Warren
Lisa D. Watson
Diana M. Weaver
Molly Weaver
Valerie Weaver
Alison Webb
Lotte D. Weimer
M. Elizabeth Weimer
Janey Wetzel
Margie Wheeler
Philip Whitmire
James Wiant
Sharon Wiant
Joan W. Wilharm
Virginia A. Wilhelm
Amy E. Williams
Sally Williams
Wanda With
Mary Wood
Phyllis M. Woods
Demitra D. Xinakes
Anne Taylor Yoo
Nancy Cutting Young
Martha Hart Yount
Michele A. Zukowski